W9-AUE-040

REDRAWING *the* MAP

The Israel-Palestine Border Conflict

KATE SHOUP

Cavendish Square
New York

Published in 2019 by Cavendish Square Publishing, LLC
243 5th Avenue, Suite 136, New York, NY 10016

Copyright © 2019 by Cavendish Square Publishing, LLC

First Edition

Library of Congress Cataloging-in-Publication Data

Names: Shoup, Kate, 1972- author.
Title: The Israel-Palestine border conflict / Kate Shoup.
Description: First edition. | New York, NY : Cavendish Square Publishing, 2019. | Series: Redrawing the map | A book for high school students about the formation of, and subsequent issues surrounding, the nation of Israel. | Includes bibliographical references and index.
Identifiers: LCCN 2018002250 (print) | LCCN 2018002600 (ebook) | ISBN 9781502635723 (ebook) | ISBN 9781502635716 (library bound) | ISBN 9781502635730 (pbk.)
Subjects: LCSH: Israel—History. | Arab-Israeli conflict—History.
Classification: LCC DS125 (ebook) | LCC DS125 .S46 2019 (print) | DDC 956.9405—dc23
LC record available at https://lccn.loc.gov/2018002250

Editorial Director: David McNamara
Editor: Erin L. McCoy
Copy Editor: Michele Suchomel-Casey
Associate Art Director: Amy Greenan
Designer: Jessica Nevins
Production Coordinator: Karol Szymczuk
Photo Research: J8 Media

The photographs in this book are used by permission and through the courtesy of: Cover Phillip Harrington/Alamy Stock Photo ; p. 5 United States National Geospatial-Intelligence Agency/Wikimedia Commons/File:Middle east graphic 2003.jpg/CCO; p. 8 Hugo H. Mendelsohn/AFP/Getty Images; p. 11 Danita Delimont/Gallo Images/Getty Images; p. 13 Fayez Nureldine/AFP/Getty Images; p. 15 Leemage/Universal Images Group/Getty Images; pp. 17, 40-41, 80, 90 Bettmann/Getty Images; pp. 20-21 Pierre Perrin/Sygma/Getty Images; p. 25 Library of Congress Prints and Photographs Division; p. 29 Unknown/Wikimedia Commons/File:Jews evacuate the Old City, 1936.jpg/CCO; pp. 34-35 Photo 12/Universal Images Group/Getty Images; p. 37 John Phillips/The LIFE Picture Collection/Getty Images; p. 45 Ralph Morse/The LIFE Picture Collection/Getty Images; p. 46 AFP/Getty Images; p. 51 Bernard Bisson/Sygma/Getty Images; p. 52 Hulton Deutsch/Corbis Historical/Getty Images; p. 54 Zero0000/Wikimedia Commons/File:BritishMandatePalestine1930s.png/CCO; p. 55 Wickey-nl/Wikimedia Commons/File:Occupied Palestinian Territories.jpg/BY-SA/3.0; pp. 60-61, 91 NurPhoto/Getty Images; p. 65 Onceinawhile/Wikimedia Commons/File:PalestineAndTransjordan.svg/BY-SA/4.0; p. 68 Zero0000A/RES/181(II)/Wikimedia Commons/File:UN Palestine Partition Versions 1947.jpg; p. 72-73 Abbas Momani/AFP/Getty Images; p. 74 David Silverman/Getty Images; p. 77 Kametaro/Shutterstock.com; p. 83 Mark Reinstein/Corbis News/Getty Images; p. 93 Mark Ralston/AFP/Getty Images.

Printed in the United States of America

CONTENTS

Chapter 1   **The Roots of the Israeli-Palestinian Conflict**   4

Chapter 2   **A Brief History of Palestine**   10

Chapter 3   **A Region Defined by Conflict**   36

Chapter 4   **Evolving Borders**   64

Chapter 5   **A Longing for Peace**   81

Chronology   95

Glossary   99

Further Information   101

Bibliography   103

Index   109

About the Author   112

CHAPTER ONE
The Roots of the Israeli-Palestinian Conflict

The region comprising modern-day Israel and Palestine—sometimes called the Southern Levant—bridges the continents of Europe, Asia, and Africa and is part of a larger region called the Middle East. As such, it is a place where cultures, commerce, and politics often collide. Much of the Southern Levant is unforgiving land—desert covers more than half of it—and yields little in the way of natural resources such as oil or minerals. Despite this, the Southern Levant has been among the most fought-over regions on Earth for the last hundred years.

There are many reasons for this volatility. Perhaps the most significant is that three major religions were born in the Southern Levant: Judaism, Christianity, and Islam. The followers of all three of these religions view the region, and especially the city of Jerusalem, as

Israel and Palestine (*at center, in green*) sit at the crossroads of Europe, Asia, and Africa.

a holy land. Two of these groups—Jews and Muslims—also believe that their religion grants them a legitimate claim on this land.

Claims on a Holy Land

The Jewish people cite the Hebrew scriptures as proof of their right to occupy Israel and Palestine. This holy book—which Christians call the Old Testament—tells the story of an Israelite named Abraham to whose descendants God granted the Southern Levant. According to these scriptures, God blessed Abraham's wife, Sarah—then ninety years old—with a child. After the birth of this child, who was named Isaac, God told Abraham, "I will establish my covenant with him as an everlasting covenant for his descendants after him." Because of this declaration, Jews (and, by extension, Christians) believe they are the descendants of Abraham through Isaac.

Muslims hold a similar belief. They, too, contend that they are descendants of Abraham. But according to their holy book, called the Qur'an, they do not descend from Isaac. Rather, they descend from Isaac's older brother, Ishmael, whose mother was Sarah's handmaid. Muslims believe that God's promise pertained not to the descendants of Isaac, but to the descendants of Ishmael—that is, to them.

Although both Jews and Muslims consider themselves to be the sole heirs to the Holy Land, they peacefully coexisted there for more than a millennium. That changed during and after World War I (1914–1918). Great Britain—charged with managing the region (now called Palestine) after the war—made conflicting promises to both groups, effectively cleaving the two communities.

A Divided Region

Beginning in the early 1920s, tensions between Jews and Muslims in Palestine escalated. Riots in 1920, 1929, and from 1936 to 1939 resulted in the deaths of hundreds of Jews and thousands of Muslims, who in Palestine are generally Arabs—a cultural and linguistic group with origins in Syria and the Arabian Peninsula. Casualties mounted during the civil war of 1947–1948, the 1948 Arab-Israeli War, the 1967 Arab-Israeli War, the 1970 War of Attrition, and the 1973 Arab-Israeli War. Both sides continue to engage in smaller combat operations to this day.

The Jews in the region—who founded a sovereign nation called Israel in 1948—won these wars with relative ease. With each victory, Israel gained more and more territory, pushing its borders—and the Arab Muslim population who lived on the other side—farther and farther outward. The impact on these Arab Muslims—now generally referred to as Palestinians—was devastating. They lost vast tracts of land and were forced to flee to neighboring countries or to one of

Rescuers search for victims in the rubble of a building in Jerusalem during the civil war of 1947–1948.

two remaining Palestinian strongholds in the Southern Levant: the West Bank and the Gaza Strip. The plight of these Palestinian refugees remains a serious problem.

Israel's current borders—particularly the ones that isolate it from the West Bank and the Gaza Strip—are a matter of ongoing dispute among Muslims inside and

A DIVIDED POPULACE

Taken together, the population of Israel and Palestine comprises roughly thirteen million people. Of these, approximately 47 percent are Muslim and 50 percent are Jewish. These demographics shift when one examines Israel and Palestine separately. In Israel, Jews outnumber Muslims three to one, whereas Muslims outnumber Jews four to one in the Palestinian territories.

outside Palestine, as well as in the broader international community. So is the status of the Palestinian territories themselves, as they neither belong to Israel nor comprise an independent Palestinian nation.

Through the years, several attempts have been made to address the continuing conflict between Israelis and Palestinians, and to establish a lasting peace. These efforts have largely failed. After all, there's a reason this fight—which has lasted more than a hundred years—is frequently called "the world's most intractable conflict." Perhaps someday both Israelis and Palestinians will agree on the necessary terms for peace. Until then, the fight will no doubt rage on.

CHAPTER TWO

A Brief History of Palestine

Early hominids settled the area comprising the Southern Levant more than a million years ago. By 12,000 BCE, inhabitants of the area had formed one of the world's earliest societies, called the Natufian culture.

During the second millennium BCE, the Southern Levant became known as Canaan. It consisted of several city-states, including one called Jerusalem. Other groups soon settled in the region, including the Philistines. Historians believe the name "Palestine" derives from the word "Philistine."

The Emergence of New Religions

Around 1200 BCE, a new group appeared in the Southern Levant: the Israelites. Israelites—also known as Jews—developed their own monotheistic religion,

The ancient city of Jerusalem is depicted in an etching.

called Judaism, and spoke their own language,
called Hebrew.

The Hebrew scriptures tell the story of the Jews
in the Southern Levant. According to this collection
of texts, Israelites established their own state—called
the United Kingdom of Israel—in the region in 1020
BCE. Later, this kingdom split in two. Starting around
750 BCE, a series of different empires absorbed
the land comprising these two kingdoms: first the

Assyrian Empire, then the Babylonian Empire, the Persian Empire, the Greek Empire, and finally, the Roman Empire.

During this tumultuous period, thousands of Jews were expelled from their homeland and traveled to other parts of the globe, particularly Europe. This mass migration came to be known as the Jewish Diaspora. Many of those who had been forced to leave longed to return to Palestine. To them, it was a holy land.

Meanwhile, during Roman rule in the Southern Levant, another religion that would come to dominate the region emerged. Around the year 4 CE, a Jew named Jesus of Nazareth was born. Jesus became an important religious leader. His followers believed he was the Son of God and founded a new religion based on his teachings: Christianity.

Sometime around 33 CE, the Romans executed Jesus. After his death, Christianity slowly grew in popularity. During the fourth century, the Roman Empire itself embraced Christianity. All its subjects—including those in the Southern Levant—were forced to worship the Christian god. It remained the official religion in the region until 634 CE.

Because the Southern Levant was the home of Jesus and his early followers, Christians all over the world came to view the land as a holy place, just as the Jews did.

The people of Jerusalem are depicted in an architrave panel of a tempietto from the first half of the eleventh century. The city at this time was diverse, and its population included both Muslims and Jews.

The Rise of Islam in the Southern Levant

In the year 634, Palestine fell to a new power: the Rashidun Caliphate. This caliphate was led by adherents of a new religion called Islam, which was based on the teachings of a prophet named Muhammad. At the time, most followers of Islam, called Muslims, descended from tribal people called

In the thirteenth century, a Turkish tribal leader named Osman seized control of a region called Anatolia. This conquest marked the beginning of the Ottoman Empire, which would overthrow the Byzantine Empire in 1453 and, at its height, control much of southeast Europe and parts of central and eastern Europe, western Asia (including the Southern Levant), the Caucasus, and northern Africa—some 2 million square miles (5.2 million square kilometers) in all. At the heart of the empire was the wealthy and cosmopolitan capital city of Constantinople. (Now called Istanbul, it is the largest city in modern Turkey.)

These vast land holdings granted the Ottomans control of the overland trade routes between Europe and the East. As a result, the empire was both prosperous and sophisticated. It was also remarkably stable. One reason for this stability was the (mostly) peaceful transfer of power between members of a single ruling family—descended directly from Osman—for more than six centuries. Another was these leaders' ability to build strong alliances across political, religious, and racial groups. Yet another was the empire's strong military, described by historians Mesut Uyar and Edward J. Erickson as "armies composed of vast numbers of soldiers, giant cannons, and bombards, relentless [infantry] warriors, and swarms of reckless auxiliary soldiers."

In 1683, the Ottoman Empire tried—but failed—to conquer the European city of Vienna. Many historians view this military failure as the beginning of the Ottoman Empire's decline. It was not the only contributor, however. The empire's waning role in international trade due to the discovery of maritime trade routes, and to emerging competition from the New World, also played a role, as did continuous pressure from neighbors with territorial designs of their own. Over time, the empire contracted in size—although it maintained its hold on the Southern Levant until the 1900s.

The Ottoman Empire is depicted in a map circa 1570. Parts of the empire are depicted by small red structures.

Arabs who hailed from the southern and eastern parts of modern-day Syria.

The Southern Levant remained under Muslim control until 1099, when Christian soldiers from Europe conquered the city of Jerusalem. This event, the first of several crusades to rid the region of Muslim rule, resulted in the formation of the Kingdom of Jerusalem. Christian rule was relatively brief, however. Muslim forces toppled the Christian kingdom in 1187. Muslim leaders went on to rule the Southern Levant for the next 735 years—first the Ayyubid dynasty, then the Mamluk dynasty, and finally, the Ottoman Empire.

Jews in Europe

Jews in the Southern Levant enjoyed relative security under Muslim rule. This was not the case for Jews in Europe. During the Middle Ages, European Jews faced near-constant persecution by Christians. Between 1290 and 1497, the governments of England, France, Spain, and Portugal expelled all the Jews within their territories. (Jews would eventually be permitted to return to these countries, but not for hundreds of years.) Others suffered an even worse fate: during the Middle Ages, Christians slaughtered the members of hundreds of Jewish communities throughout Europe. These massacres, called pogroms, resulted in the deaths of thousands of Jewish men, women, and children.

To escape this persecution and violence, some European Jews migrated to the Southern Levant,

Many Jews in Russia were killed in pogroms during the late 1800s.

where they lived in relative peace among their Muslim neighbors. A great many more moved to eastern Europe. At first, Jews in eastern Europe enjoyed considerable freedom. Jewish society flourished. Sadly, however, this did not last. Between 1648 and 1656, pogroms resulted in the murder of as many as one hundred thousand eastern European Jews.

Territorial changes during the late eighteenth century placed millions of Jews under Russian rule. The

Russian government then imposed laws that restricted their rights. Russian Jews soon fell victim to a series of deadly pogroms. This prompted more than two million Jews to emigrate from Russia between 1881 and 1939. Many traveled to the United States. Others chose a different destination: the Southern Levant.

The Birth of Zionism

Many Jews who migrated to the Southern Levant wanted not only to purchase property and settle down, but to establish a Jewish homeland there. After all, the region—which was then under the rule of the Ottoman Empire and primarily inhabited by Muslims of Arab descent—had been the site of the ancient United Kingdom of Israel. The movement to create a Jewish state in the Southern Levant—by then popularly referred to as Palestine—was called Zionism.

Some members of the British government took a keen interest in Zionism. A British politician named Herbert Samuel summarized their stance in an influential 1915 pamphlet called "The Future of Palestine," in which he referenced the cruel anti-Semitism that pervaded Europe:

> Let a Jewish centre be established in Palestine; let it achieve … a spiritual and intellectual greatness; and insensibly, but inevitably, the character of the individual Jew, wherever he might be, would be ennobled. The sordid associations which have attached to the Jewish

name would be sloughed off, and the value of the Jews as an element in the civilisation of the European peoples would be enhanced. The Jewish brain is a physiological product not to be despised … If a body be again given in which its soul can lodge, it may again enrich the world.

The Great War and the Seeds of a Longer Conflict

July 1914 marked the advent of the Great War, later called World War I. This war pitted Britain, France, Russia, and the United States (the Allied powers) against Germany, Austria-Hungary, and the Ottoman Empire (the Central powers).

The Allied powers believed that conquering Palestine and the broader Middle East was critical to victory on the Ottoman front. To achieve this, a British official named Henry McMahon persuaded Husayn ibn Ali, emir of the holy city of Mecca, to unleash an Arab uprising against Ottoman forces. In return, McMahon promised that the British would support the creation of an independent Arab state after the war. Although McMahon was vague regarding the precise location of this future state, Husayn assumed it would include Palestine.

Husayn delivered on his end of the bargain. Accusing the Ottomans—who were of Turkish rather

Husayn ibn Ali, emir of Mecca, helped launch an Arab uprising against the Ottoman state.

than Arab ethnicity—of "impiety," he assembled an army of some seventy thousand Arab men to rebel against the Ottomans in June 1916. Just as the British had hoped, this uprising, called the 1916 Arab Revolt, turned the tide of the war in the Middle East.

The British proved less honorable than Husayn. In May 1916, they signed a secret treaty with France called the Sykes-Picot Agreement that split the Levant—of which Palestine was a part—in two. According to this treaty, France would claim one portion of the territory and Britain the other—with none of it going to the Arabs. "The Arab Revolt had begun on false pretenses," recalled British officer T. E. Lawrence, who had worked as an organizer and liaison during the uprising. "The promises to the Arabs were dead paper." About this deception, Lawrence was "continually and bitterly ashamed." This broken promise was a significant cause of the turmoil that would soon arise in the Middle East between Israel and Palestine—turmoil that continues to this day.

The other main cause of this ongoing conflict was the November 1917 Balfour Declaration. Issued by British foreign minister Lord Arthur James Balfour, it read as follows:

> His Majesty's government view[s] with favour the establishment in Palestine of a national home for the Jewish people, and will use their best endeavours

to facilitate the achievement of this object, it being clearly understood that nothing shall be done which may prejudice the civil and religious rights of existing non-Jewish communities in Palestine, or the rights and political status enjoyed by Jews in any other country.

According to historian Ali A. Allawi, "Probably no other declaration in modern times has had such an impact on entire peoples, has been so mired in controversy and has had such astounding consequences." Two significant problems arose with this declaration. First, it contradicted McMahon's promise to Husayn to create an Arab state. Second, its call for the creation of a "national home for the Jewish people" in Palestine ran contrary to the wishes of the local population—roughly 90 percent of whom were not Jewish. Complicating matters was the ambiguity of the phrase "national home." As observed by historian Robert H. Lieshout, that phrase could mean anything from a "spiritual centre for the Jews" to "a fully fledged state."

The local Arab population did not object to the presence of Jews. Indeed, as Faysal ibn Husayn, son of Husayn ibn Ali, observed, "The Jews are very close to the Arabs in blood, and there is no conflict of character between the two races ... I assert that with the Jews who have been seated for some generations in Palestine our relations are excellent." However, Arabs could not countenance the surrender of Palestinian territory to form a "national home for Jewish people"—particularly if that national home would be an independent nation. On this subject, Faysal warned: "If [the Jews] want to constitute a state and claim sovereign rights in this region, I foresee very serious dangers. It is to be feared that there will be a conflict between them and the other races [in the region]." Sadly, Faysal's fears proved prophetic.

In the end, the British faced a pivotal choice: they could deliver Palestine to the Arabs; divide the land containing Palestine between themselves and the French; or establish a Jewish homeland there. But they could not do all three. This choice, based on contradictory promises, became the root of a conflict in the Middle East that has endured for a hundred years— and for which it appears there is no end in sight.

The British Mandate for Palestine

The implementation of the Sykes-Picot Agreement and the Balfour Declaration hinged on one event: Allied victory in World War I. This came to pass in November 1918.

Starting in January 1919, leaders of the countries comprising the Allied powers held a series of meetings to establish the terms of peace. These meetings culminated in the signing of several treaties. Among these was the Treaty of Versailles.

In addition to formally ending hostilities with Germany, the Treaty of Versailles ordered the formation of an international organization called the League of Nations. The league's mission was "to promote international co-operation and to achieve international peace." The treaty also spelled out the league's charter. This included the redistribution of colonies belonging to members of the Central powers. The league deemed these colonies—which it called mandates— unable "to stand by themselves under the strenuous conditions of the modern world" and determined that their administration should be "entrusted to advanced nations who by reason of their resources, their experience or their geographical position can best undertake this responsibility … until such time as they are able to stand alone." These "advanced nations," called mandatories, would not own the mandates assigned to them. Rather, they would administer them on behalf (though not under the control) of the League of Nations.

In 1922, per the terms of the Sykes-Picot Agreement, the League of Nations split the Levant into two mandates: the French Mandate for Syria and the Lebanon and the British Mandate for Palestine. (The British also took control of another mandate: the British Mandate for Iraq.)

Churchill Weighs In

In 1921, the British government had appointed a politician named Winston Churchill to the position of colonial secretary. Churchill's job was to untangle the morass created in Palestine due to Britain's conflicting promises to the Jews, the Arabs, and the French.

Winston Churchill (*left*) is pictured in Palestine with T. E. Lawrence (*center*) and Abdullah ibn Husayn.

Churchill's solution was to partition the Palestinian mandate along the Jordan River. Land west of the river, which would retain the name of Palestine, would remain under direct British authority and constitute the Jewish homeland. Land to the east would become its own entity, called Transjordan, and would be placed under Arab rule (although it would remain a British mandate). The British installed Abdullah ibn Husayn, another son of Husayn ibn Ali, as emir of Transjordan and appointed Faysal ibn Husayn emir of the British Mandate for Iraq. (Both Iraq and Transjordan would gain complete independence in the coming years—Iraq in 1932 and Transjordan, later renamed simply Jordan, in 1946.)

This solution, said Lawrence, "made straight all the tangle" in the region and fulfilled all the promises made by the British "in letter and spirit." In other words, it seemed to make good on McMahon's promise to Husayn to create an Arab state, while also accommodating the demands of both the Balfour Declaration and the Sykes-Picot Agreement. Arabs and Jews saw things differently, however. Arabs were upset because they considered Palestine to be holy ground, and as such, believed it should remain under Muslim rule. Jews were likewise upset that the holy land, which they believed included Transjordan, would not belong to them in full.

Growing Tension

At the end of the Great War, Faysal ibn Husayn and a Jewish leader named Chaim Weizmann attempted to lay the groundwork for peaceful coexistence among Arabs and Jews in Palestine by hammering out an agreement. This agreement was issued before Churchill's partition of Palestine and therefore assumed that Britain would allow for the formation of an independent Arab state that would encompass a Jewish homeland (though not a

Jewish state) in Palestine. It declared first and foremost that "the Arab State and Palestine in all their relations and undertakings shall be controlled by the most cordial goodwill and understanding."

Sadly, any hope for amiable relations between Arabs and Jews in the region quickly vanished. By 1920, relations had broken down to such an extent that a four-day riot erupted in Jerusalem, killing five Jews and four Arabs. Another riot in 1921—this one lasting eight days—consumed the city of Jaffa, killing forty-seven Jews and forty-eight Arabs.

In a 1922 white paper, the British government attributed this increasing tension to apprehensions among both Arabs and Jews about the Balfour Declaration. Arab concerns were "partly based upon exaggerated interpretations of the meaning of the declaration favouring the establishment of a Jewish national home in Palestine." In contrast, Jewish anxieties were rooted in concerns that the British government might "depart from the policies embodied in the declaration."

To reassure the Arab population, the white paper affirmed that "the terms of the declaration ... do not contemplate that Palestine as a whole should be converted into a Jewish national home, but that such a home should be found 'in Palestine.'" It also affirmed Britain's commitment to preventing "the disappearance or subordination of the Arabic population, language or customs in Palestine" and "the imposition of

CHANGING DEMOGRAPHICS

In 1878, more than 15,000 Jews lived in Palestine, comprising roughly 3 percent of the total population. By the end of 1936, that number had grown to an estimated 384,000. More than 200,000 Jews arrived in Palestine between 1931 and 1936 alone.

Jewish nationality upon the inhabitants of Palestine as a whole."

To soothe the Jewish population, the white paper affirmed that "the declaration … is not susceptible to change" and that "the Jewish community in Palestine should be able to increase its numbers by immigration"—although this immigration could not be "so great in volume as to exceed whatever may be the economic capacity of the country to absorb new arrivals"; it added that "immigrants should not be a burden upon the people of Palestine."

A Boiling Point

Britain's 1922 white paper had acknowledged the importance of limiting Jewish immigration to Palestine to avoid overwhelming the region. Nevertheless, over the next several years, thousands upon thousands of Jews immigrated there. Indeed, by 1936, Jews comprised almost 30 percent of the total population of Palestine, up from just 9 percent in 1920.

For many Palestinians, this continuing influx of Jewish immigrants posed a serious threat. "The Arabs," observed one Jewish leader, David Ben-Gurion, were

Jews evacuate Jerusalem following the Arab riots in 1936.

"fighting dispossession … The fear is not of losing land, but of losing the homeland of the Arab people, which others want to turn into the homeland of the Jewish people." This fear sparked more violence. In 1929, Arabs massacred 67 Jews in the city of Hebron. Later that year, a series of riots in Jerusalem resulted in the deaths of 133 Jews and 110 Arabs. On and on the violence went—triggered sometimes by one side, sometimes by the other.

In late 1935, British agents assassinated a key Palestinian militant. In retaliation, Palestinians launched a general strike. This quickly deteriorated into acts of vandalism and violence against Jewish settlers. The result was a cycle of terror exacerbated by both sides—a cycle that would last, on and off, until 1939.

Rather than remain neutral in this conflict, the British government sided with the Jews. As many as 50,000 British troops coordinated with some 15,000 Jewish militants to violently suppress the Arab rebellion. Between 1936 and 1939, more than 5,000 Arabs died—far greater than the number of Jews (300) or Britons (262).

Of the seemingly never-ending bloodshed in Palestine, one British officer observed, "The Jew murders the Arab and the Arab murders the Jew … This is what is going on in Palestine now. And it will go on for the next fifty years in all probability."

In fact, it would go on for much longer than that.

A Change in Policy

Britain eventually became, says historian Tom Segev, "sick of Palestine." He explains: "As the Arab protest continued, as terrorism increased, and as the winds of war began to blow in Europe, the growing feeling in London and among the British in Jerusalem was that Palestine had become a burden there was no longer any reason to bear."

Britain established a new policy in Palestine in May 1939. The White Paper of 1939 acknowledged the legitimacy of Arab grievances. As one politician put it, the British government had in fact *not* been "free to dispose of Palestine without regard for the wishes and interests of the inhabitants of Palestine" in the aftermath of World War I.

The new policy called for three significant changes to Britain's approach to Palestine. First, it ordered the formation of an independent Palestinian state, governed by both Jews and Arabs, within the next ten years. Second, it curtailed Jewish immigration to seventy-five thousand people over the next five years and, following that period, the cessation of Jewish immigration altogether unless by Arab consent. This was to address "the fear of the Arabs that this influx [of Jewish immigrants] will continue indefinitely until the Jewish population is in a position to dominate them." Finally, it restricted the transfer of land from Arabs to Jews to enable "Arab cultivators ... to maintain their existing standard of life" and to prevent the creation of "a considerable landless Arab population."

A Zionist organization called the Jewish Agency for Israel issued a stern rebuke of this policy. The group stated that "the Jewish people regard this policy as a breach of faith and a surrender to Arab terrorism," that the policy "denies to the Jewish people the right to rebuild their national home in their ancestral country," and that it "transfers the authority over Palestine to the present Arab majority and puts the Jewish population at the mercy of that majority."

The Jewish Agency also criticized the policy's timing. This was an allusion to a development in Europe that had placed Jews in great danger: the ascension of Adolf Hitler and his Nazi regime in Germany. Under Hitler, Jews in Germany and in other

Nazis hold Jews at gunpoint in the Warsaw, Poland, ghetto in 1943. The Nazis tried to completely exterminate the Jewish people in a campaign they called the Final Solution.

territories seized by the Nazis had faced growing anti-Semitism. By 1939, the Nazis had boycotted Jewish businesses; burned books written by Jews; barred Jews from serving in the German military; banned Jews from holding civil-service, government, or university positions; stripped Jews of their citizenship; barred Jews from practicing medicine; expelled Jews from German schools; and forced Jews to register their property.

The Nazis also openly encouraged violence against Jews. This triggered a pogrom in November 1938. During this attack, called Kristallnacht (Night of the Broken Glass), Nazis ransacked thousands of Jewish homes, businesses, schools, and synagogues, and murdered at least ninety-one Jews. They also arrested some thirty thousand Jewish men and imprisoned them in concentration camps. Britain's new policy, issued "in the darkest hour of Jewish history ... to deprive the Jews of their last hope and to close the road back to their homeland" was, the Jewish Agency said, "a cruel blow."

Palestinian Arabs were likewise unhappy with Britain's new policy, but for a different reason: they felt it didn't go far enough. Arab leaders weren't satisfied with limiting Jewish immigration; they wanted its complete and total prohibition. They also wanted Britain to renounce the notion of a Jewish homeland in Palestine. Nevertheless, unlike Jewish leaders—who rejected the policy outright—Arab leaders ultimately supported it.

World War II and the Holocaust

In October 1939—just five months after Britain issued its new policy for Palestine—Germany successfully invaded Poland. This marked the beginning of World War II, during which Germany, Italy, and Japan (the Axis powers) clashed with Britain, France, the Soviet Union, and the United States (the Allied powers).

For the Germans, the acquisition of territory was a key objective. Poland was just one of its many conquests. Germany had already appropriated Austria and Czechoslovakia and would later seize Denmark, Norway, the Netherlands, Belgium, Luxembourg, France, Greece, and Yugoslavia. However, expanding its borders wasn't Germany's only goal. Another was the complete extermination of the Jewish people—a murderous campaign it called the Final Solution and that the rest of the world later called the Holocaust or the Shoah (Hebrew for "destruction").

During the Holocaust, Nazis slaughtered Jews in a methodical and merciless manner. Indeed, in some concentration camps, they murdered as many as eight thousand Jews a day. By the end of the war in 1945, the Nazis had massacred some six million European Jews—about two-thirds of all Jews in Europe. Roughly one-quarter of these were children.

CHAPTER THREE
A Region Defined by Conflict

After World War II, evidence mounted of the anti-Semitic atrocities the Nazis had committed during the conflict. In response to these horrifying revelations, many Jews in Palestine became openly anti-British. Some even engaged in guerrilla warfare with British troops or performed acts of vandalism or sabotage. They believed Britain's anti-immigration policies, as outlined in the White Paper of 1939, had stranded countless Jews in Europe and prevented them from escaping death at the hands of the Nazis.

Fueling this fire was Britain's continued enforcement of strict immigration quotas in Palestine. Hundreds of thousands of surviving European Jews—most of whom had suffered terribly in concentration camps—had been displaced by the war. A considerable majority of these sought to migrate

A seven-year-old girl in Jerusalem flees during the civil war of 1947–1948 as the buildings behind her burn.

to Palestine. However, the British refused to let them in. Unthwarted, many European Jews attempted to enter Palestine illegally. Some succeeded, but many more failed. These unlucky individuals found themselves once again interned in camps—this time by the British.

Their plight turned public opinion against Britain worldwide. This widespread censure, coupled with the seemingly never-ending violence in Palestine, prompted Britain to release its mandate on Palestine at last. For guidance with this transition, Britain turned to the United Nations (UN), which had formed in 1945 to succeed the League of Nations. The UN assembled a special committee called the United Nations Special Committee on Palestine (UNSCOP) to study the matter.

The UNSCOP quickly grasped that any plan it devised would need to accommodate both Jewish and Arab interests. It would also need to tackle the plight of Jews displaced by the Holocaust. To achieve these aims, the UNSCOP proposed the partition of Palestine to create two independent states—one Arab and one Jewish. The latter would be free to accommodate increasing numbers of Jewish immigrants. The committee also proposed the placement of Jerusalem under international control. In late 1947, the UN officially adopted this plan, and Britain set the mandate's expiration date to May 15, 1948. The region, unfortunately, would not know peace for many decades, as the UNSCOP's proposal could not prevent escalating violence and territorial conflicts that would leave tens of thousands dead in the coming years and would uproot many more.

Public reaction to the UNSCOP plan was mixed. Jews were generally in favor of it, while Arabs were overwhelmingly opposed. Arabs, who constituted the majority in Palestine, argued that the partition of Palestine violated their right to self-determination—a key piece of the UN charter—and warned that its implementation would result in widespread bloodshed throughout the Middle East. "Partition imposed against the will of the majority of the people will jeopardize peace and harmony in the Middle East," one Iraqi official observed. "Not only the uprising of Arabs of Palestine is to be expected, but the masses in the Arab world cannot be restrained." An Egyptian official concurred, noting that if Palestine were to be partitioned, "no force on earth could prevent blood from flowing there" and that "no force on earth can confine it to the borders of Palestine itself." The official added, "Jewish blood will necessarily be shed elsewhere in the Arab world."

War in Palestine

Warnings issued by Arab leaders quickly proved prescient. Indeed, on November 30, 1947—just one day after the UN's official adoption of the UNSCOP plan—eight Arab men attacked two buses near a Jewish settlement and killed seven passengers. Three days later, an Arab mob armed with clubs and knives killed eight Jews and burned numerous Jewish-owned buildings in Jerusalem. These attacks marked the beginning of a civil war in Palestine.

"On paper and on the ground," observes writer David Margolick, "the [Arabs] had the edge: there were twice as many of them, they occupied the higher altitudes and they had friendly regimes next door." But, Margolick continues, "isolated and outnumbered as they were, the Jews were far better organized, motivated, financed, equipped and trained than their adversaries." Once the Jews went on the offensive, they effectively nullified the UNSCOP plan by capturing all the territory that had been allotted to them, and then some.

Israel Declares Independence

On May 14, 1948, one day before the expiration of the British mandate, members of the Jewish National Council—formed in 1920 to handle Jewish communal affairs in Palestine—gathered to sign a declaration of independence on behalf of all Jews in Palestine. The declaration called for "the establishment of a Jewish state in Eretz-Israel [the land of Israel], to be known as the State of Israel."

Israel, the declaration affirmed, would "foster the development of the country for the benefit of all its inhabitants," would be "based on freedom, justice and peace as envisaged by the prophets of Israel," would "ensure complete equality of social and political rights

Israeli leaders declare independence on May 14, 1948.

to all its inhabitants, irrespective of religion, race or sex," would "guarantee freedom of religion, conscience, language, education and culture," and would "safeguard the Holy Places of all religions." The new state would also be "open for Jewish immigration and for the ingathering of exiles."

The declaration petitioned "the Arab inhabitants of the State of Israel to preserve peace and participate in the upbuilding of the state on the basis of full and equal citizenship and due representation in all its provisional and permanent institutions," extended Israel's hand "to all neighbouring states and their peoples in an offer of peace and good neighbourliness," and appealed to them "to establish bonds of cooperation and mutual help with the sovereign Jewish people settled in its own land." Finally, the declaration vowed that Israel was "prepared to do its share in a common effort for the advancement of the entire Middle East."

One topic the declaration conspicuously avoided was where the borders for this new state should be drawn. This was because Jewish leaders held opposing views on where those borders should fall. Some sought to establish Israel's borders in accordance with the UNSCOP plan. Others clung to the notion that the Jews should claim all of Palestine—even the part now held by Jordan. Still others argued that the borders should be set according to gains made by Israeli fighting forces during the civil war. Finally, in September 1948, Israel's provisional government passed a law reflecting this last position, giving Israel the right to claim all land it had acquired—or might acquire—during its ongoing conflict with the Arabs, both then and in the future.

Several countries, including the United States and the Soviet Union, recognized the newborn state of Israel almost immediately. Arab nations were less welcoming (with the exception of Iran, which acknowledged Israel within a matter of days). Indeed, several Arab states—including Egypt, Jordan, and Iraq, as well as Syria and Lebanon (which had gained their independence from France in the mid-1940s)—were "compelled to intervene for the sole purpose of restoring peace and security and establishing law and order in Palestine." These Arab states, which comprised a coalition called the Arab League, argued that "the only fair and just solution to the problem of Palestine is the creation of [a] United State of Palestine based upon the democratic principles."

The 1948 Arab-Israeli War and the Palestinian Exodus

Just one day after Israel declared independence, four Arab states—Egypt, Lebanon, Jordan, and Syria—escalated the ongoing civil war by attacking the new state of Israel. "Underestimating the power of the fledgling state, Arab rulers thought they were heading towards an easy victory," reports Al Jazeera. In fact, the Arab states "suffered a humiliating defeat at the hands of the Israeli military." Within a matter of months, Israeli fighters—who had quickly coalesced into a national army, called the Israeli Defense Force (IDF)—pushed back Arab combatants, claiming yet more territory for Israel.

However, there were two areas the IDF didn't capture. One was a region west of the Jordan River called the West Bank; this included East Jerusalem. Jordan had occupied this land during the fighting and chose to keep it for itself. The other was a sliver of

David Ben-Gurion, born David Gruen, played an important role in the formation of Israel.

Ben-Gurion was born on October 16, 1886, in the Polish city of Plonsk. His father was a Zionist leader. In 1906, Ben-Gurion migrated to Palestine. Soon after he arrived, he helped build the region's first kibbutz, or communal settlement. Ben-Gurion also engaged in political activities to promote Jewish independence in Palestine—including helping to establish a Jewish defense organization.

During World War I, Ben-Gurion's Zionist political activities prompted Ottoman leaders to expel him from Palestine. Ben-Gurion traveled to New York City, where he met a Russian émigré named Pauline Munweis. The couple married and raised three children.

Britain gained control of Palestine in the waning months of the Great War. In 1917, it issued the famous Balfour Declaration, which called for the formation of a "Jewish national home" in the region. Ben-Gurion—who was now free to return to Palestine—viewed this as an important first step to Jewish independence in the region.

Another important step toward independence was the foundation of the Jewish National Council in 1920 by Jewish leaders in Palestine—including Ben-Gurion. That same year, Ben-Gurion also established a labor union for Jewish workers in the region. In 1930, he helped found a new political party, which he subsequently led. And between 1935 and 1946, Ben-Gurion became leader of two other important Jewish organizations: the Jewish Agency and the World Zionist Organization.

As the head of several Jewish organizations, Ben-Gurion was instrumental in writing and issuing Israel's declaration of independence. Indeed, it was he who broadcast the contents of the declaration in a radio address on May 14, 1948. After the formation of the Israeli government, Ben-Gurion became a key member: he served as Israel's first prime minister and first minister of defense— positions he held from 1949 until 1953, and again from 1955 to 1963. Finally, Ben-Gurion served in the Knesset—Israel's House of Representatives— from 1949 to 1970.

David Ben-Gurion was a key figure in the formation of Israel.

During Ben-Gurion's tenure as prime minister, Israel built up its military; passed the Law of Return, which gave Jews everywhere the right to settle in Israel; absorbed and assimilated hundreds of thousands of Jews from all over the world (some seven hundred thousand during the country's first three years); built an excellent public education system; established new towns and cities in outlying areas; and built a national water system, among other accomplishments.

Upon his retirement from government service, Ben-Gurion moved to a kibbutz called Sde-Boqer, where he wrote multiple memoirs and published several speeches, essays, and letters.

David Ben-Gurion died on December 1, 1973, in the city of Tel Aviv. But his legacy endures. As noted by Israeli historian Michael Bar-Zohar, Ben-Gurion's "charismatic personality won him the adoration of the masses, and, after his retirement from the government and, later, from the Knesset ... he was revered as 'Father of the Nation.'"

Mediterranean coastline called the Gaza Strip, which had been captured by Egypt.

The fighting of 1947 and 1948—which had been triggered by the prospect of Israeli statehood—drove as many as seven hundred thousand Palestinian Arabs from their land and homes. During this exodus, often called the Nakba (Arabic for "disaster"), most Palestinians fled to the West Bank or Gaza Strip (collectively referred to as the Palestinian territories). Others escaped to neighboring Arab countries. Hundreds of thousands of these refugees settled in camps where conditions were crowded, housing was primitive, and jobs were scarce. Later, the Knesset passed laws that denied these refugees the right to return to Israel and reclaim their land.

"The founding of Israel," observes one faculty member at Columbia Law School, "rendered the Palestinians a stateless people who retained a sense of national identity, but were dispersed across a broad range of jurisdictions—mirroring in a tragic way the status of the Jewish people prior to the founding of the state of Israel." Palestinian refugees weren't citizens of Israel—or of any other nation on Earth.

The Lausanne Protocol and the Green Line

Starting in early 1949, Israel signed a series of agreements with Egypt, Lebanon, Jordan, and Syria to end the fighting and to establish an armistice line. This line—which would be monitored by the UN and

A Palestinian refugee woman and her child are pictured in 1948, separated from their home by the Green Line.

enforced by the United States, Britain, and France—was called the Green Line. The placement of the Green Line corresponded not with the borders set by the UNSCOP partition plan, but rather with the cease-fire line. That is, the Green Line reflected Israel's territorial gains during the civil war of 1947–1948 and the 1948 Arab-Israeli War.

The Green Line was not intended to be a permanent border. It was meant to serve as an interim line until the "Palestine question" could be settled following further negotiations. In 1949, the UN facilitated these negotiations—which, in addition to covering the issue of a permanent border, also dealt with the problem of Arab refugees who had been driven from their homes during the war,

Israel's stance on the refugee situation was, in the words of historian Avi Shlaim, "clear and emphatic: the Arab states were responsible for the refugee problem, so responsibility for solving it rested with them." (Even so, Israel *was* willing to make a financial contribution to expedite matters.) As for the border issue, Shlaim writes, "Israel's position was that the permanent borders between itself and its neighbors should be based on the cease-fire lines, with only minor adjustments."

On both points, the Arab contingent disagreed. Concerning the refugee problem, Arab leaders sought from Israel the "repatriation of the refugees and payment of due compensation for their lost or damaged property, as well as for the property of those who do not wish to return"—this according to a document submitted to the UN. Regarding the border, Arab leaders pushed for a return to the UNSCOP partition plan.

Ultimately, the Arabs accepted the partition of Palestine, and both parties signed an agreement to that effect. Soon, however, it became clear that the Israelis had signed the agreement—called the Lausanne Protocol—simply to ensure that the UN would accept Israel as a member state. Once that happened, says historian Ilan Pappé, Israel "retreated from the protocol it had signed, because it was completely satisfied with the status quo, and saw no need to make any concessions with regard to the refugees or on boundary questions."

Israel's refusal to adhere to the terms of the Lausanne Protocol made peace an impossibility. As a result, Israelis and Palestinians continued to skirmish over the next several years. Sometimes Israel was the aggressor. This was the case in October 1953, when more than a hundred Israeli troops entered the West Bank and slaughtered forty-two Arabs. Other times, it was the Arabs who launched the attack—for example, in March 1954, when Arab fighters ambushed a bus carrying Jewish passengers and murdered eleven people on board.

The Suez Crisis

In July 1956, Egypt seized control of the Suez Canal from France and Great Britain. Egypt then barred Israeli vessels from the 120-mile (193-km) waterway, which connected the Mediterranean Sea to the Red Sea. Egypt also prohibited Israeli ships from entering the Straits of Tiran, which joined the Gulf of Aqaba to the Red Sea. This effectively denied Israel access by sea to the east.

In response, Israel coordinated with France and Britain to attack Egypt. Israel moved quickly, capturing the Sinai before its allies even had a chance to mobilize. Bowing to pressure from the UN and the United States, all parties quickly agreed to a cease-fire. The terms of this agreement called for Egypt to reopen the Suez

Canal and Straits of Tiran to Israeli ships, for Israel to withdraw from the Sinai, and for the UN to deploy peacekeeping troops to the Sinai.

Israel no doubt lamented its surrender of the precious territory it had gained during the crisis. However, the Israeli government had discovered something even more valuable: it did not need military support from Allied nations to conquer the Sinai. It could do it all on its own. This knowledge would factor heavily into Israeli military strategy in the years to come.

The Ascent of the Palestine Liberation Organization

In 1964, pro-Palestine activists formed a new group called the Palestine Liberation Organization (PLO). The PLO's stated mission was the "complete liberation of Palestine, and eradication of Zionist economic, political, military and cultural existence" primarily through "armed public revolution" (although the organization would also employ diplomatic channels). The PLO also demanded the return of all Palestinian refugees to their homes.

At first, Israel and other members of the international community considered the PLO, which was led by Yasser Arafat, to be a terrorist organization. Over time, however, their stance evolved. In November 1974, the UN granted the PLO observer (though not member) status in the organization and affirmed for Palestinians the "right to self-determination

Palestine Liberation Organization leader Yasser Arafat speaks at a press conference during his visit to the European Parliament in 1988.

without external interference," the "right to national independence and sovereignty," and the "right to return to their homes and property." In 1993, Israel declared it would, in the words of then prime minister Yitzhak Rabin, "recognize the PLO as the representative of the Palestinian people" and would "commence negotiations with the PLO within the Middle East peace process."

Israeli troops survey an Egyptian aircraft destroyed by the Israeli offensive on the Sinai during the Third Arab-Israeli War.

The 1967 Arab-Israeli War

In June 1967, Israel's growing confidence in its military after the Suez Crisis would prove well founded. Over the course of just six days, Israel defeated Arab enemies on three sides—in Egypt, Jordan (reinforced by Iraqi fighters), and Syria. It also defeated Palestinians in the West Bank and Gaza Strip.

This conflict—called the Third Arab-Israeli War or the Six-Day War—had been set in motion by the Soviet Union, which had falsely informed Egypt that Israel was gathering troops on the Syrian border. Historians disagree as to whether this was simply a blunder or part of a deliberate disinformation campaign. Either way, on May 19, 1967, Egypt expelled the UN peacekeepers who had been installed in the Sinai to enforce the post-Suez cease-fire, assembled its own troops in the region, and once again closed the Straits of Tiran to Israeli vessels.

For Israel, this closure of the Straits of Tiran constituted a casus belli. It quickly marshaled its own military forces. Before Egypt and its allies (which included Jordan, Iraq, and Syria) could strike, Israel launched a surprise air attack on the Sinai on June 5, 1967, and effectively destroyed the Egyptian air force. Subsequent attacks on the Jordanian air force and the Syrian air force later that day proved similarly successful. Thanks to these attacks, Israel would enjoy near-total air supremacy for the duration of the war.

In the following days, Israel won battle after battle. As Arab fighters beat a hasty retreat, Israel captured considerable territory beyond the Green Line—territory that had previously fallen under Jordanian, Syrian, and Egyptian control. Israeli forces relented only after all sides agreed to a cease-fire on June 11.

The cease-fire ended the Third Arab-Israeli War, but it did not bring a lasting peace—despite Israeli efforts to secure one. On June 19, the Israeli government

During the Third Arab-Israeli War, Israel seized the Gaza Strip and the Sinai Peninsula from Egypt; the West Bank, including East Jerusalem, from Jordan; and an area called the Golan Heights from Syria. This more than tripled the amount of land under Israeli control. Later, Israel returned the Sinai to Egypt and annexed East Jerusalem and the Golan Heights for itself. The West Bank and the Gaza Strip remained disputed territory. They are neither Palestinian nor Israeli (although effectively controlled by Israel), and their inhabitants are citizens of nowhere.

Israel's acquisition of East Jerusalem placed the Old City—including the Temple Mount—under Jewish control for the first time in two millennia. This was a bitter loss for Arab Muslims, however, for whom the Temple Mount—which they call Haram al-Sharif—is also holy. Both Israelis and Arabs continue to clash over who rightfully controls these and other holy sites in Jerusalem and around Israel.

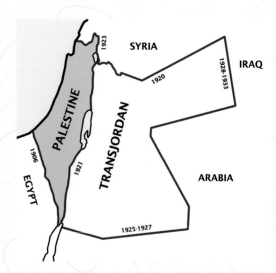

The borders drawn by the British Mandate for Palestine were in effect between 1923 and 1948.

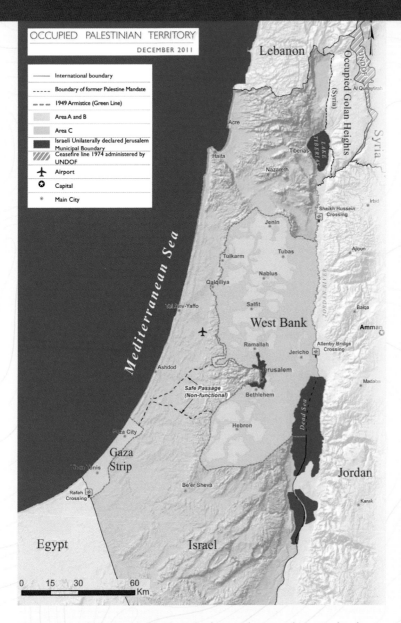

The borders of Israel and Palestine are shown above as they stand today.

A DEADLY CONFLICT

More than 20,000 Arab troops were killed in action during the Third Arab-Israeli War, and as many as 325,000 Arab civilians were displaced. Fewer than 1,000 Israeli fighters lost their lives.

voted to surrender the Sinai (but not the Gaza Strip) and the Golan Heights to Egypt and Syria, respectively, in exchange for peace. Arab leaders, however, were unmoved. An official Egyptian radio broadcast conveyed the Arab position, declaring that there could be "no peace with Israel, no survival of the influence of imperialism and no existence in our land of the Zionist state."

Hostilities between Arabs and Israelis quickly resumed. These initially took the form of small-scale attacks. Tensions escalated in March 1969, when Egypt again declared war on Israel. This conflict—which later drew the participation of Egyptian allies including Jordan, the Soviet Union, and the PLO—lasted until the US government orchestrated a cease-fire in August 1970. As before, Israel emerged victorious from this conflict—called the War of Attrition—sustaining fewer casualties than its enemies and retaining all the territory it had claimed in 1967. But again, it had not secured a lasting peace.

Nor did a subsequent war—called the Fourth Arab-Israeli War—result in a resolution. This conflict began on October 6, 1973, when Egypt and Syria coordinated a surprise attack on Israel on Yom Kippur, a Jewish holy day. The Israeli military, caught completely off guard, struggled to mobilize. This gave Arab forces an early advantage. The tide soon turned, however. Israeli forces pushed Arab fighters back to the boundaries established during the Third Arab-Israeli War, resulting in a cease-fire on October 25.

The Intifadas

Even when the Arabs and the Israelis were not officially at war, the violence between them continued. On and on it went: Arabs attacking Jews and Jews attacking Arabs—each confrontation more brutal than the last. Much of this violence clustered in two key areas: the West Bank and the Gaza Strip.

The vast majority of Arabs in Israel—having been displaced from their homes during the 1948 and 1967 Arab-Israeli wars—lived in the West Bank and the Gaza Strip. Although the populations of both of these areas were overwhelmingly Palestinian, they remained under Israel's control—although the Israeli government did eventually delegate certain administrative tasks to Palestinian officials. Palestinians resented this arrangement and regarded Israel as an occupying force.

By the late 1980s, the West Bank and the Gaza Strip had become tinderboxes, just waiting for a spark to ignite them. That spark came on December 9, 1987, when an Israeli Jeep collided with a van carrying several Palestinian workers in the Gaza Strip. Four workers died. Historians differ on whether this incident was planned or just an accident. Either way, writes historian

Sonja Karkhar, for many Palestinians, it was the last straw "in a twenty-year saga of military occupation and its debilitating effects on a population denied any control over their economic, social and political development." The Palestinians rose up in rage.

This uprising—called the First Intifada—lasted for almost four years. Palestinians conducted strikes and boycotts, erected barricades, scrawled graffiti, and threw stones and Molotov cocktails at Israeli forces. Israel's response was severe. In the first year of the First Intifada, Israeli soldiers killed 311 Palestinians—53 of whom were under the age of seventeen.

Thanks to various peace efforts during the early 1990s, the First Intifada eventually petered out. But the failure of those peace efforts reignited hostilities in 2000. This time, Palestinians did not limit themselves to relatively minor acts of vandalism and violence. Rather, they conducted scores of suicide bombings in Israeli territory. These attacks targeted Jews wherever people congregated—in restaurants and nightclubs, crowded streets, and buses.

One suicide bombing killed twenty-eight Israelis celebrating Passover at a resort. This proved a turning point for Israel's then–prime minister Ariel Sharon. "The Palestinians must be hit, and it must be very painful," he said afterward. "We must cause them losses, victims, so that they feel a heavy price." Israel's retributive campaign involved military raids on Arab civilians and the assassination of several key Palestinian leaders. Nearly five hundred Palestinians—many of them children—were killed.

Changes in the Palestinian Territories

During the Second Intifada, fighting in the Gaza Strip between Palestinians and Israeli forces was particularly fierce. To extricate itself, Israel unilaterally withdrew from Gaza in 2005, granting all control of the area—except for the borders, airspace, and territorial waters—to the Palestinians. This arrangement continues today.

To reduce Palestinian violence against Israelis, Israel also built a security barrier along the segment of the Green Line demarcating the Gaza Strip boundary. This barrier severely restricted the movement of both people and goods in and out of Gaza—effectively segregating Gazans from the rest of Israel and the outside world. A similar barrier was erected along the West Bank soon thereafter (although it went beyond the Green Line to encroach on Palestinian territory).

These security barriers did reduce Palestinian violence against Israeli civilians. However, they also cut off many of those Palestinians who worked on the other side of the wall from their livelihoods. As a result, the economies of the Palestinian territories plummeted—particularly in Gaza. According to the World Bank, "the blockade in place since 2007 has shaved around 50 percent of Gaza's [gross domestic product]. Unemployment in Gaza is the highest in the world at 43 percent. Even more alarming is the situation

Pro-Palestinian protestors clash with Israeli forces guarding the border wall near Gaza City on December 15, 2017. The protestors are voicing their opposition to US president Donald Trump's recognition of Jerusalem as the capital of Israel.

of youth unemployment which soared to more than 60 percent by the end of 2014."

These circumstances have forced many Palestinians in Gaza into poverty. As observed by the World Bank, their misery is compounded by "poor access and quality of basic public services such as electricity, water, and sewerage," not to mention a lack of nutritious food. The situation in the Palestinian territories is without question a humanitarian crisis—and the crisis is still growing today.

Palestinian Statehood and the PNA

On November 15, 1988—more than forty years after

Israel claimed statehood—the PLO issued Palestine's own declaration of independence. At the core of the Palestinian declaration was this passage:

> The occupation of Palestinian territory and parts of other Arab territory by Israeli forces, the uprooting of the majority of Palestinians and their displacement from their homes by means of organized intimidation, and the subjection of the remainder to occupation, oppression and the destruction of the distinctive features of their national life, are a flagrant violation of the principle of legitimacy and of the Charter of the United Nations and its resolutions recognizing the national rights of the Palestinian people, including the right to return and the right to self-determination, independence and sovereignty over the territory of its homeland.

The UN recognized Palestine's declaration of independence in December 1988. In 2012, it upgraded Palestine's status from "observer entity" to "non-member observer state." This was an implicit acknowledgment of statehood but did not endow Palestine with full membership in the UN, as Palestinian officials had requested.

The Palestinian National Authority (PNA) was established to govern this state in 1994. It handles civilian affairs in the West Bank and Gaza. The PNA does not, however, claim sovereignty over these areas; they remain disputed territories.

The PNA is led by a president and a prime minister (who in turn commands a cabinet of officials). It also has a legislative body called the Palestinian Legislative Council (PLC). Since the establishment of the PNA, several political parties have formed in Palestine. These include Hamas and Fatah; the latter is associated with the PLO.

Palestinian Civil War

In 2006, the Hamas party—a militant group whose charter called for the invalidation of Israel—dealt a surprising electoral defeat to the more moderate Fatah party to claim a majority in the PLC. This triggered a Palestinian civil war in the Gaza Strip between Hamas fighters and Fatah forces—a fight that resulted in the deaths of more than six hundred Palestinians. Not only were inhabitants of the Gaza Strip caught in the cross fire of this internecine war, they also faced increasing aerial bombardments by the Israeli military, which stepped up operations in response to the ascension of Hamas.

Hamas eventually overwhelmed its Fatah rivals and seized complete control of Gaza. This effectively split the Palestinian territories into two separate domains— the Gaza Strip (governed by Hamas) and the West Bank (governed by Fatah). In 2014, both parties agreed to the formation of a united government, but tension between Fatah and Hamas remains—and it is only exacerbated by their ongoing conflict with Israel.

CHAPTER FOUR
Evolving Borders

Before the League of Nations endowed Great Britain with the Mandate for Palestine in 1922, the geographical and territorial limits of the region were poorly defined. Palestine was, in the words of *Encyclopædia Britannica*, "a nebulous geographical concept."

Palestine's boundaries might have been nebulous prior to British mandate, but its ownership was not. It had been held by the Ottoman Empire for more than six hundred years. Although the Ottomans had not demarcated boundaries for the region in its entirety, they had divided it into administrative entities called *vilayets* (provinces) and *sanjaks* (districts). When the British redrew the borders in 1923, they encompassed the southern portions of the vilayets of Syria and Beirut and the sanjaks of Jerusalem, Nablus, and Acre.

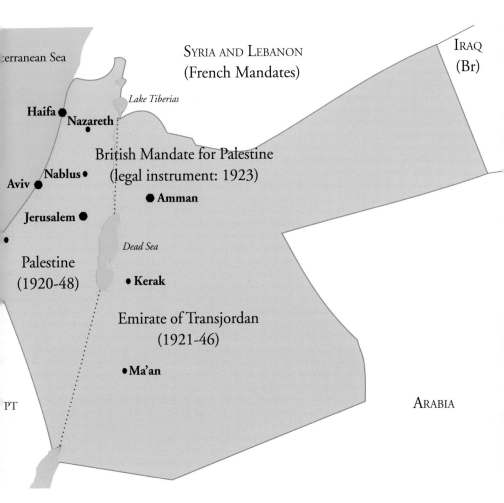

The British Mandate for Palestine drew new borders in the region.

The French Mandate for Syria and the Lebanon
bordered the British Mandate for Palestine to the north.
This border was simply administrative in nature. That
is, it was not marked by specific geographical features—
although mapmakers did place several key railways
and waterways in British territory. To the east lay the

British Mandate for Iraq and a tribal area now called Saudi Arabia. The borders between the Palestinian mandate and these areas—characterized by a vast and unrelenting desert—were the result of international agreements rather than geographical features. As such, they were essentially straight lines. So, too, was the border separating the Palestinian mandate from the sovereign nation of Egypt—although this line crossed a variety of terrain, ranging from rugged mountains to fertile plains. Only Palestine's western border was defined by a geographical feature: the Mediterranean Sea. Within these boundaries lay important water sources, including Lake Hula, the Jordan River, and part of the Yarmouk River.

At the urging of Winston Churchill, Britain split the Palestinian mandate in two in 1924. The Jordan River served as the boundary between the two regions. The land east of the river became Transjordan (later shortened to simply Jordan), an Arab state. The land to the west retained the name Palestine and was intended to serve as the Jewish homeland. The same year, Britain surrendered an area called Golan Heights to the French Mandate for Syria. In exchange, the French gave the northern portion of the Jordan Valley, including the Sea of Galilee, to Britain.

Failed Borders

When the British government moved to release the Palestinian mandate in 1947, it turned to the United

Nations for guidance. The UN determined that the best approach would be to partition Palestine into two independent states—one Arab and one Jewish—and to place Jerusalem under international rule. This plan, the UN hoped, would go into effect upon the British withdrawal from Palestine. However, it would prove to be just one of many disputed border changes in the years to come.

To devise the borders for these proposed new states, the UN considered only one data point: demographics. That is, it determined where Jewish populations were highest and cobbled those areas together to create a Jewish state, relegating the Arab state to the rest of the territory, wherever that may be. This explains why the resulting map took on what the Jewish Virtual Library calls "a checkerboard appearance."

The UN plan allotted the Arab state all the highlands (except Jerusalem) and one-third of the Mediterranean coastline. Altogether, this territory—which comprised about 43 percent of Mandatory Palestine—would house some 725,000 Arabs and 10,000 Jews. For the Jewish state, the UN plan allocated three fertile lowland plains, two-thirds of the Mediterranean coastline, and the Negev Desert (which, at that time, was not suitable for agriculture or urban development), as well as sole access to the Red Sea and the Sea of Galilee. This region comprised about 56 percent of Mandatory Palestine and would be home to some 498,000 Jews and 407,000 Arabs.

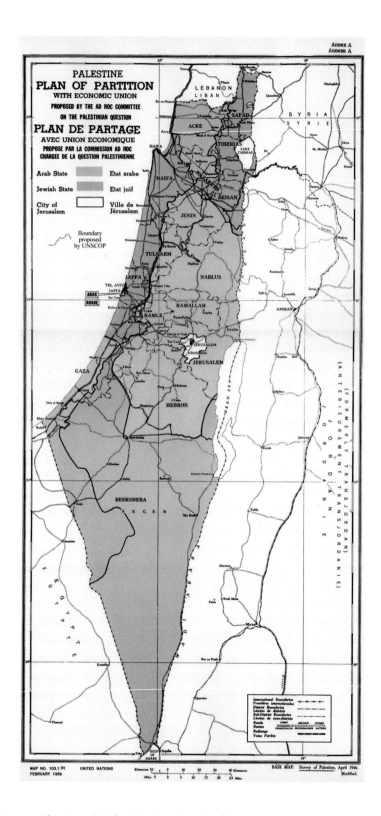

TERRITORIAL SIZES

Israel covers 8,019 square miles (20,770 sq km). It stretches 263 miles (424 km) from north to south. At its widest point, Israel is 71 miles (114 km) across. At its narrowest point, it is just 9.3 miles (15 km) wide. The Palestinian territories cover 2,313 square miles (5,993 sq km). The West Bank encompasses 2,172 square miles (5,628 sq km), while Gaza comprises just 140 square miles (365 sq km). These two Palestinian territories are not connected.

status of the West Bank and Gaza Strip was a subject of considerable dispute. Israel contended it had earned control of these areas through its successful efforts during the 1967 war. Palestinians—and much of the international community—disagreed. The status of both regions remains unsettled even today.

Settlements and Barriers

Even as the status of the Gaza Strip and the West Bank remains unclear, Israel has constructed dozens of settlements in both areas since its victory in the 1967 war. These settlements are communities populated almost entirely by Jewish civilians, and they are heavily subsidized by the Israeli government.

There were two main reasons for the construction of these settlements. First, says journalist Frank Jacobs, "the secular state sought effective ways to pacify (or at least control) the occupied territories." Second, "A fundamentalist element in Israeli society considered

Palestinian workers pass through a checkpoint between the Palestinian West Bank and the Jewish settlement of Modi'in Illit.

living in these newly conquered areas a religious right, if not a duty." Some religious leaders shared this belief. "The world's redemption," wrote Orthodox rabbi Avraham Kook, "depended on the Jews living in the Land of Israel"—*all* the land of Israel.

These settlements are not uniform in character. Some are nothing more than small outposts housing perhaps a few hundred settlers. Others are farming communities. Some are villages, and some are urban suburbs. Finally, some—such as Ariel, Betar Illit, Ma'al Adumim, and Modi'in Illit—are full-blown cities. The largest of these, Modi'in Illit, houses some sixty-six thousand residents—mostly ultra-Orthodox Jews—and boasts fifty schools, eighty synagogues, extensive public transportation, and a large shopping mall.

The Palestinians regard the continued construction of these settlements as a provocation. The international community agrees. UN Security Council Resolution 2334, passed in 2016, calls Israeli settlements a "flagrant violation" of international law and says they have "no legal validity." The resolution asserts that the settlements are a violation of the Fourth Geneva Convention, which states that "the Occupying Power shall not deport or

WATER RESOURCES

Although the distribution of land is the main cause of the Israeli-Palestinian conflict, water rights also play a role—and have for the last fifty years.

After the Third Arab-Israeli War, Israel seized complete control over the region's three main sources of natural freshwater, including two vast underground aquifers that flow beneath both territories. Israel's stranglehold on the water supply only tightened with its construction of the security barriers in Palestinian territories. As explained by Amnesty International, "The route of the [barrier] has been planned in such a way that it prevents access by Palestinians to areas … which include some of the best access to water."

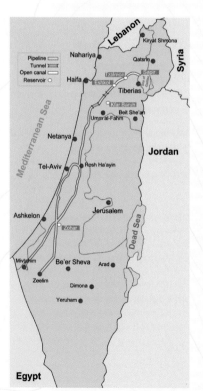

Thanks to Israel's control over the water supply, Israelis receive much more water than Palestinians—8,475 cubic feet (240 cubic meters) per person per year, compared to 4,414 cubic feet (125 cu m) for Palestinians in the Gaza Strip and 2,648 cubic feet (75 cu m) for those in the West Bank. This water is often polluted.

In July 2017, Israel agreed to sell Palestine an additional 32 million cubic feet (906,139 cu m) of water per year. This may alleviate the current water crisis, but it won't solve it. There will be no solution, says Palestinian Water Authority president Mazen Ghoneim, "unless Israel's occupation ends and we get our water rights in the underground basins that Israel controls."

Israel's control of the region's water supply has created a water crisis in Palestine.

transfer parts of its own civilian population into the territory it occupies."

Even some Israelis agree with this stance. Indeed, in 1967, Theodor Meron, an advisor to the Israeli prime minister, said, "My conclusion is that civilian settlement in the administered territories contravenes the explicit provisions of the Fourth Geneva Convention." In 2007, Meron reiterated this position, asserting that "the fact that settlements were established and the pace of the establishment of the settlements made peacemaking much more difficult."

Still, about half a million Israelis live in the roughly 130 settlements scattered across the West Bank. (Israel dismantled all settlements in Gaza in 2005.) "As a result," says Jacobs, "what's left of the occupied territories for the Palestinians looks less like the contiguous mini-nation it could be, and more like a bizarre, landlocked archipelago."

Security Barriers

To shield itself from Palestinian violence, Israel built security barriers between it and the Gaza Strip and West Bank. These barriers are, says Middle East expert Dan Rothem, "comprised of an electronic fence surrounded by a detection path, patrol road, ditch, and barbed wires" in some areas, and in others, "a stark concrete wall."

The barriers—which Palestinians often call the apartheid wall or the annexation wall—are the source of a great deal of conflict. Rothem explains: "The controversy surrounds the route of the barrier, which deviates from the 1967 lines (the only lines of Israeli sovereignty recognized by the international community) and includes the three large settlement blocs and their surroundings." What's more, the barriers rob thousands of Palestinians of access to their families and livelihoods on the Israeli side of the fence.

The International Court of Justice (ICJ) agrees. As reported by journalist Chris McGreal, the ICJ "condemned what it described as the widespread confiscation and destruction of Palestinian property, and the disruption of the lives of thousands of protected civilians, caused by construction of what Israel calls the 'anti-terror fence.'" The ICJ's ruling stated, in its own words, that the construction of the barrier "cannot be justified by military exigencies or by the requirements of national security or public order," and that "the construction, along with measures previously taken ... severely impeded the exercise by the Palestinian people of its right to self-determination." Finally, the ICJ called on the UN to "consider what further action is required to bring to an end the illegal situation resulting from the construction of the wall and the associated regime." The Israeli government hotly contested this ruling—its theory being that the wall serves to protect Israeli civilians—with one aide claiming that the report would "find its place in the garbage can of history."

A security barrier separates Israel and the West Bank.

The Distribution of Natural Resources

As Israel has adjusted its borders over the years through the construction of settlements and the erection of the security barriers, it has absorbed various natural resources from the Palestinian territories. It has also maintained control of certain resources within these occupied territories, including port access, arable land, water, and more.

Among the geographic advantages that Israel enjoys is access to three seaports: the Port of Haifa and the Port of Ashod on the Mediterranean, and the Port of Eliat on the Red Sea. In contrast, Palestine has just one seaport—the Port of Gaza—which has not been operational since 2007, when Israel imposed a naval blockade on Gaza. This lack of access to sea-based trade routes has made it more difficult for Palestinians to grow their economy.

Arable land is another sticking point. Not only has Israel confiscated much of the land best suited for agriculture in the Palestinian territories, it has increased water prices for those few Palestinian farmers who remain. Israel has also imposed a variety of other obstacles designed to limit the success of these farmers, such as the prohibition of certain pesticides (which Israeli farmers are permitted to use) and delays at barrier checkpoints. In addition to damaging the Palestinian economy, these obstacles reduce food security in the Palestinian territories. Because of this, many Palestinians go hungry.

Proposed Borders for a Future Palestinian State

Proponents of peace hope that Israel and Palestine will accede to the formation of a Palestinian state. If this occurs, both parties will need to agree to the boundaries of this new state—on the Gaza side and on the West Bank side.

The border between Israel and Gaza is fairly well set—especially since Israel's unilateral withdrawal from the area in 2005. As for the border on the West Bank, there are a few options on the table. One option would place the boundary along the security barrier. Another is to transfer control over a region called the Triangle, which runs adjacent to the Green Line, to the Palestinians in exchange for settlements along the border. A third option, favored by Palestinian leaders, is to return to "pre-1967 borders"—that is, to the borders as they stood before the Third Arab-Israeli War.

Which of these options—if any—will be chosen remains to be seen.

CHAPTER FIVE
A Longing for Peace

Even as the violence between Palestinians and Israelis has continued in a seemingly never-ending cycle, parties on both sides of the struggle have worked toward peace. These peace efforts began in earnest after the Fourth Arab-Israeli War in 1973. Although Israel had prevailed in this conflict, victory had been more difficult to achieve than in 1948 and 1967. This caused Israel's confidence in its military supremacy to waver. Palestinians' reaction to the 1973 war was the exact opposite. Their early military successes during the war gave them a psychological boost. However, they also concluded from the outcome of the war that Israel could not be defeated militarily. These insights by both parties placed them on a path to peace—although this path would prove perilous.

Opposite: During the Geneva Conference of 1973, the empty seats were meant for representatives from Syria, which, along with the Palestine Liberation Organization, boycotted the conference.

Efforts Toward Peace

The first step on this path to peace was the Geneva Conference, assembled in December 1973 by the UN. Attendees included representatives from Egypt, Jordan, and Israel (although not Syria or the PLO), along with top officials from the United States and the Soviet Union. The goal of the conference was the implementation of UN Resolution 242. This resolution—drafted (but not implemented) after the Third Arab-Israeli War—cited the "inadmissibility of the acquisition of territory by war and the need to work for a just and lasting peace in the Middle East in which every state in the area can live in security." It also called for the "withdrawal of Israeli armed forces from territories occupied in the recent conflict" in exchange for "termination of all claims or states of belligerency and respect for and acknowledgment of the sovereignty, territorial integrity and political independence of every state in the area and their right to live in peace within secure and recognized boundaries free from threats or acts of force." Finally, the resolution reiterated the necessity of "achieving a just settlement of the refugee problem."

The opposing parties failed to reach an agreement regarding the details of Resolution 242 during the Geneva Conference. However, they did agree that the resolution could serve as a basis for addressing the Arab-Israeli conflict in the future and that it provided a useful map to peace.

Resolution 242 would inform nearly all subsequent peace negotiations between Israel, its Arab neighbors, and the PLO (as well as global partners like the United States and the Soviet Union). Negotiations in 1974 brought about Israel's military disengagement with Egypt and Syria. Negotiations in 1975 resulted in the Sinai Agreement, which declared that future conflicts between Egypt and Israel would "not be resolved by military force but by peaceful means." In 1978, negotiations resulted in the Camp David Accords. These set the stage for a treaty between Egypt and Israel in 1979, in which Israel returned the Sinai to Egypt in exchange for a lasting peace. Negotiations in 1983 brought peace between Israel and Lebanon.

The 1993 signing of the Oslo Accords by Israel and the PLO after the First Intifada represented a significant leap forward on the path to peace. These accords called for Israel's gradual release of its control over the Gaza Strip and portions of the West Bank (excluding Jerusalem) to the PNA. In return, the PLO would recognize Israel's right to exist and renounce its desire for Israel's annihilation. After signing the accords, Israel's then–prime minister, Yitzhak Rabin, remarked, "We who have fought against you, the Palestinians, we say to you today, in a loud and a clear voice, enough of blood and tears. Enough."

This thawing of Israeli-Palestinian relations cleared the way for yet more agreements and treaties. A 1994 agreement led to Israel's withdrawal from the city of

From left, Israeli prime minister Yitzhak Rabin, US president Bill Clinton, and Palestine Liberation Organization leader Yasser Arafat gather to sign the 1993 Oslo Accords.

Jericho, in the West Bank, and from most of the Gaza Strip. That same year, a peace treaty between Israel and Jordan formally ended hostilities between those two states. And a 1997 agreement ceded a portion of the city of Hebron, also in the West Bank, to Palestinian control.

Perhaps the best hope for a lasting peace was the Arab Peace Initiative, issued in 2002 and reaffirmed in 2007 and in 2017. This initiative—crafted and endorsed by the Arab League—called for Israel's "complete withdrawal from the occupied Arab territories … to the 4 June 1967 line," a move that the Arab League considered "a just solution to the problem of Palestinian refugees." The goal would be "the establishment of an independent and sovereign Palestinian state … in the West Bank and Gaza Strip with East Jerusalem as its capital." In return, members of the Arab League would "consider the Arab-Israeli conflict over, sign a peace agreement with Israel, and achieve peace for all states in the region," as well as "establish normal relations with Israel within the framework of this comprehensive peace." As observed by UN leader Ban Ki Moon, this initiative "[sent] a clear signal that the Arabs are serious about achieving peace." Nevertheless, Israel rejected the initiative. This

GLOBAL RECOGNITION OF PALESTINE

As of September 2015, 136 of the 193 member nations of the UN had recognized the state of Palestine. So has the International Olympic Committee, which permits the participation of Palestinian athletes in the Olympic Games. Israel, however, has not recognized it.

rejection, writes Israeli journalist Akiva Eldar, represents Israel's "worst missed opportunity."

Possible Solutions

Most peace efforts have focused on a two-state solution. This approach calls for the formation of a sovereign Palestinian state—likely comprising the West Bank and the Gaza Strip—to coexist with Israel. According to one 2013 poll, 52 percent of Israelis, 70 percent of Palestinians in the West Bank, and 48 percent of Palestinians in the Gaza Strip support a two-state solution. Unfortunately, observed the editors at the *Economist* in 2009, "there have been precious few moments over the past century during which both sides have embraced the idea of two states at the same time." What's worse, "with the rise of Hamas and the war in Gaza, the brief period of relative hope is in danger of flickering out."

A two-state solution is not the only possible solution, however. Another option is a one-state solution. Under this approach, explains Palestinian-American law professor George Bisharat:

> Israel/Palestine should have a secular, bilingual government elected on the basis of one person, one vote as well as strong constitutional guarantees of equality and protection of minorities, bolstered by international guarantees. Immigration should follow nondiscriminatory criteria. Civil marriage between members of different ethnic or religious groups should

Young Palestinians demonstrate during a 2015 rally in Gaza City organized by a women's branch of Hamas.

be permitted. Citizens should be free to reside in any part of the country, and public symbols, education and holidays should reflect the population's diversity.

Some hard-line Palestinians, such as members of Hamas, also support a one-state solution—although they envision a single Islamic state free of Jews. This is, obviously, a nonstarter for Israel. However, support for the one-state solution described by Bisharat is growing.

There's even a three-state solution. In this scenario, as described by former US ambassador to the UN John R. Bolton, "Gaza is returned to Egyptian control and the West Bank in some configuration reverts to Jordanian sovereignty." In other words, the region would return to the status maintained from 1949 until 1967. Bolton continues: "Having the two Arab states re-extend their prior political authority is an authentic way to extend the zone of peace and, more important, build on governments that are providing peace and stability in their own countries." This solution has gained little traction, however.

Of course, there remains the option of maintaining the status quo. Some Israelis support this solution—the theory being, writes philosophy professor Raja Halwani, that it might "exhaust the Palestinians, wear them down, and eventually get them to lower their expectations and demands, if not to altogether leave the region." However, Halwani argues, "occupying a population, appropriating its lands, targeting its civilians, and so on are examples of immoral actions, actions that would remain immoral even if some good came out of them." Indeed, Bisharat observes that the status quo—which he describes as "permanent Israeli rule over disenfranchised Palestinians"—is "tantamount to apartheid." Nathan Thrall of the International Crisis Group offers another reason to eschew the status quo: "The status quo isn't stasis—it's steadily making it more difficult to withdraw in the future, and certainly making it more costly to withdraw." This makes it "the most frightening of the possibilities."

New York Times columnist Thomas Friedman frames the possible solutions to the Israeli-Palestinian conflict differently. He argues that Israel has three simple options: to be "a nation of Jews living in all the land of Israel, but not democratic"; "a democratic nation living in all the land of Israel, but not Jewish"; or "a Jewish and democratic nation, but not in all the land of Israel." It must choose one of these.

Barriers to Peace

Since the Second Intifada (2002) and the ascent of Hamas (2006), peace efforts have slowed, but they have not stopped. Meetings are still conducted, terms negotiated, cease-fires issued, and peace proposals submitted. Still, it often seems as if the barriers to peace are insurmountable.

Perhaps the most challenging obstacle pertains to the distribution of land. "At heart, this is a struggle of two peoples for the same patch of land," observe the editors of the *Economist*. Assuming Israel and Palestine implement a two-state solution, they must agree on the placement of the borders between them, who keeps control of the holy city of Jerusalem, whether Palestinian refugees will be permitted to return to their land in Israel, and what will become of Jewish settlements in the West Bank.

For guidance on this issue, peacemakers have turned to UN Resolution 242, but each side of the conflict interprets the terms it lays forth differently—particularly the language of the clause calling for the "withdrawal of Israeli armed forces from territories occupied in the recent conflict" (referring to the Third Arab-Israeli War). Because this clause does not specify that "all" or even "the" recently occupied territories should be vacated, many Israelis have interpreted it to

CONFLICT OVER JERUSALEM

For Jews, Muslims, and Christians, the city of Jerusalem is a holy place. This makes it a particular point of contention for Israelis and Palestinians.

Interestingly, most early Zionists were secular Jews, "motivated more by concerns about nationalism, self-determination and escape from persecution than by religious visions," reports Mona Boshnaq, alongside other writers and experts, in the *New York Times*. According to Jewish scholar Amnon Ramon, these Jews "recoiled from Jerusalem, particularly the old city." Professor Michael Dumper agrees, noting that "Jerusalem was something of a backwater, a regression to a conservative culture that they were trying to move away from." Over time, however, their desire for control over Jerusalem grew.

To skirt this conflict, the 1948 UN plan placed Jerusalem under international control. The formation of Israel and the 1948 Arab-Israeli War prevented the implementation of this plan, however. Instead, Jerusalem was partitioned according to the 1949 armistice line, with Israel holding West Jerusalem and East Jerusalem falling to the Palestinians.

Jerusalem remained divided until the Third Arab-Israeli War, when Israel seized East Jerusalem. The emotional impact of this

development proved intoxicating. "Images of Israeli soldiers praying at the Western Wall, to which they had been denied access during Jordanian rule, became seared into Israel's national consciousness," observes Boshnaq. For their part, Palestinians viewed the loss of East Jerusalem as a catastrophe.

Israeli soldiers pray at the Western Wall following the Israeli victory in the Third Arab-Israeli War.

The international community has condemned Israel's occupation of East Jerusalem. UN Security Council Resolution 478 called it "a violation of international law." Nevertheless, in 1980, Israel's Knesset declared that "Jerusalem, complete and united, is the capital of Israel." In 2000, Palestine passed a similar law, claiming Jerusalem for itself.

For nearly forty years, the entire international community withheld recognition of Jerusalem as the capital of Israel (or of Palestine). All but two countries maintained their embassies in the city of Tel Aviv. (Those two countries—Costa Rica and El Salvador—moved their embassies to Tel Aviv in 2006.) That changed in December 2017, when US president Donald Trump announced the relocation of the American embassy to Jerusalem—"upending decades of US diplomacy and threatening to spark a massive unrest across the Muslim world," journalists Jennifer Williams and Sarah Wildman observe. "Israel is a sovereign nation with the right like any other sovereign nation to determine its own capital," Trump argued. "Acknowledging this is a fact is a necessary condition for achieving peace."

Most Middle East experts disagree. Following Trump's announcement, Williams and Wildman report, the PLO ambassador to Washington called Trump's decision "a knife in the back," and Palestinians burned pictures of Trump and the Israeli flag. Perhaps more than ever, a lasting peace in the region seems elusive at best.

Palestinians in Gaza protest US president Donald Trump following his 2017 decision to move the US embassy to Jerusalem.

mean that a partial withdrawal is acceptable. Some also contend that Israel fulfilled this obligation in 1978, when it returned the Sinai to Egypt. The Palestinians disagree with this position.

However, according to the editors of the *Economist,* the conflict is "much less tractable" than a simple land dispute. "It is also about the periodic claim of each side that the other is not a people at all—at least not a people deserving sovereign statehood in the Middle East." This dehumanization of the "other" has proved terribly damaging to the peace process. Journalist Bryan E. Frydenburg observes, "Until far more Israelis and Palestinians see each other as fellow humans who have suffered in this conflict and see their own side is far from blameless, expect little to change except for the worse." Sadly, Israel's erection of security barriers in the West Bank and the Gaza Strip has only decreased the likelihood of Israelis and Palestinians seeing each other "as fellow human beings." This, says scholar Christine Leuenberger, is because the barriers have caused "a decline in the possibility of interacting with each other, of getting to know each other"—resulting in "an increased possibility of people stereotyping and demonizing each other."

Searching for Hope

The ongoing conflict between Israel and Palestine is often described as "intractable," or impossible to solve. This, says Israeli writer Amos Oz, is because the

Palestinian and Israeli girls socialize during an annual program designed to build bridges between the two populations.

conflict is "a clash between right and right … [and] sometimes, recently … between wrong and wrong." In other words, both sides have a legitimate claim on the land comprising modern-day Israel and Palestine, but it seems neither is willing to compromise. Both sides want peace—but only on *their* terms.

"If people are pro-Israel, they are pro-Israel one-hundred-and-twenty percent," Oz observes. The same is true of people who are pro-Palestinian. Bridging this divide is impossible. For this reason, Oz suggests reframing the conflict. "I don't think a decent person has to choose between being pro-Israel and pro-Palestinian. I think you have to be pro-peace."

A pro-peace stance requires compromise, regardless of which side of the conflict you're on. In the words of the editors of the *Economist*, Israel must ultimately "show not only that it is too strong to be swept away but also that it is willing to give up the land … where the promised Palestinian state must stand." For their part, Palestinians must lay down their arms and accept Israel's right to exist.

Perhaps someday both parties will adopt this stance and make the compromises necessary to ensure a lasting peace. Until that happens, it seems the situation will continue just as it is—and may even become worse.

CHRONOLOGY

- **1200 BCE** The Israelites emerge in the Levant.

- **750 BCE** The Jewish Diaspora begins.

- **136 BCE** Jews are expelled from most of the Levant.

- **1187 CE** Muslims begin to rule the Levant. The last of these will be the Ottomans, whose rule will end in 1922.

- **1209** The expulsion of Jews across Europe begins in England and continues in France (1306), Spain (1492), and Portugal (1497). Many Jews move to eastern Europe.

- **1880** Increasing anti-Semitism in Europe and rising Zionism prompt more European Jews to migrate to Israel in the coming decades.

- **1914** World War I begins. The war will bring about the collapse of the Ottoman Empire.

- **1915** British official Henry McMahon promises Arab leader Husayn Ibn Ali that the British will support the creation of an independent Arab state in Palestine if Husayn unleashes an Arab uprising against Ottoman forces. Husayn will deliver on his end of the bargain in 1916. McMahon, ultimately, will not.

- **1916** Britain signs the Sykes-Picot Agreement with France, calling for the Levant to be split between the French and the English.

• **1917**   The British issue the Balfour Declaration, which calls for the creation of a Jewish homeland in Palestine.

• **1922**   The British Mandate for Palestine is formed.

• **1933**   Jews in Europe begin a three-year period of mass migration to Israel following Adolf Hitler's ascension to power in Germany.

• **1936**   Arabs launch a three-year revolt against the British mandate.

• **1939**   Great Britain limits Jewish immigration to Palestine.

• **1939**   World War II begins. It will bring about the Jewish Holocaust.

• **1947**   Great Britain announces its intention to release the Palestinian mandate.

• **1947**   On November 29, the United Nations (UN) proposes the partition of Palestine into a Jewish and a Palestinian state. Palestine devolves into civil war.

• **1948**   Israel declares its independence on May 14. On May 15, the British mandate ends and the Arab-Israeli War of 1948 begins. Egypt, Syria, Lebanon, and Jordan invade Israel the same day.

• **1949**   Israel signs armistice agreements with Egypt, Jordan, Lebanon, and Syria, and the UN establishes the Green Line as an interim border for Israel.

- **1956** The Suez Crisis heightens tensions between Israel and Egypt.

- **1964** The Palestine Liberation Organization (PLO) forms.

- **1967** The Third Arab-Israeli War begins on July 5. In just six days, Jews capture significant territory beyond the Green Line—including Egypt's Sinai Peninsula.

- **1969** The War of Attrition between Israel and Egypt begins in March. It will continue through August 1970.

- **1973** Israel fights Egypt and Syria in the Fourth Arab-Israeli War, which takes place October 6-25.

- **1974** Israel and Egypt agree to militarily disengage in January. Israel and Syria agree to militarily disengage in May.

- **1979** Israel and Egypt sign a peace agreement on March 26. Israel returns the Sinai to Egypt.

- **1983** Israel and Lebanon sign a peace agreement on May 17.

- **1987** In December, the First Intifada begins, and Hamas is founded.

- **1988** Palestine declares independence on November 15.

CHRONOLOGY

• 1993 Israel and the PLO sign the Oslo Peace Accords on September 13.

• 1994 Israel and Jordan sign a peace treaty on October 26.

• 2000 The Camp David II Summit fails.

• 2000 The Second Intifada begins in September, and the region descends into violence once again.

• 2002 The Arab League puts forth the Arab Peace Initiative. Israel rejects it. The Arab League reaffirms the initiative in 2007 and 2017.

• 2015 Violence escalates between Palestinians and Israelis in September and October.

• 2017 In May, Hamas declares its willingness to accept borders in accordance with pre-1967 boundaries.

annex To appropriate territory for one's own use.

anti-Semitism Prejudice against Jewish people.

aquifer An underground water source.

armistice line The line where fighting has stopped at the end of a war.

caliphate An area ruled by a Muslim leader.

casus belli A justification for war.

charter A written description of an organization's mission and function.

covenant An agreement.

emir The title granted a Muslim ruler.

Diaspora The dispersal of Jews from Israel during ancient times.

exodus The departure of a large group of people from one region to another.

internecine A conflict between members of a single group.

intractable Difficult, stubborn, or hard to solve.

kibbutz A communal settlement (typically a farm) in Israel.

majority A group in a country, region, or territory that is more populous than another.

mandate In this case, a commission from the League of Nations to administer another territory.

minority A group in a country, region, or territory that is less populous than another.

monotheistic The belief that there is only one god.

pogrom An attack on a specific ethnic group (often Jews).

provisional government An interim government that oversees an area until a formal government can be established.

secular Describes someone or something that is not religious in nature.

sovereign Describes a country that possesses self-determination.

suicide bombing A bomb attack carried out by someone who intends to kill himself or herself, along with other people.

white paper A government report.

Zionism A movement promoting the settlement of the Southern Levant by Jews.

Books

Barakat, Ibtisam. *Tasting the Sky: A Palestinian Childhood*. New York: Farrar, Straus and Giroux, 2007.

Friedman, Thomas. *From Beirut to Jerusalem*. New York: Anchor, 1990.

Oz, Amos. *A Tale of Love and Darkness*. New York: Mariner Books, 2005.

Sacco, Joe. *Palestine*. Seattle, WA: Fangtagraphics, 2001

Zenatti, Valerie. *When I Was a Soldier*. London, UK: Bloombury, 2007.

Websites

Historical Timeline: 1900–Present—History of the Israeli-Palestinian Conflict
israelipalestinian.procon.org/view.timeline.php?timelineID=000031

A comprehensive timeline outlines important moments in the conflict, each with descriptions written by authoritative sources.

Key Documents for Understanding the Arab-Israeli Conflict
masshumanities.org/ph_key-documents-for-understanding-the-arab-israeli-conflict

This article provides a succinct introduction to each of the important documents that came to define key moments in the conflict over the last century.

Nine Facts About the Israel-Palestine Conflict on Which We Can All Agree
www.huffingtonpost.com/qasim-rashid/9-israel-palestine-facts_b_5643077.html

Qasim Rashid, a human rights attorney and visiting fellow at Harvard University's Prince Al Waleed bin Talal School of Islamic Studies, outlines key points of agreement in a century-long disagreement.

Videos

The Conflict Zone
www.nationalgeographic.org/media/israel-palestine-conflict-zone

National Geographic explains both sides of the Israeli-Palestinian conflict.

Guide: Why Are Israel and the Palestinians Fighting Over Gaza?
www.bbc.co.uk/newsround/20436092

These videos offer an introduction to the geography of the region, a history of the Gaza conflict, and a report on children in the Gaza Strip.

Promises
www.pbs.org/pov/promises

This documentary seeks to show what it's like to live in Jerusalem by hearing what seven children, both Israeli and Palestinian, think about the conflict in their region.

BIBLIOGRAPHY

Al Jazeera. "Why the Arabs Were Defeated." July 13, 2009. http://www.aljazeera.com/focus/arabunity/2008/02/200852518398869597.html.

Allawi, Ali A. *Faisal I of Iraq*. New Haven, CT: Yale University Press, 2014.

Amnesty International. *Troubled Waters—Palestinians Denied Fair Access to Water*. Amnesty International Publications, 2009. https://www.amnestyusa.org/pdf/mde150272009en.pdf.

Ariel Center for Policy Research. "The Charter of the Hamas." August 18, 1988. http://www.acpr.org.il/resources/hamascharter.html.

Balfour, Arthur James. "Balfour Declaration 1917." Yale Law School, 1917. http://avalon.law.yale.edu/20th_century/balfour.asp.

Bar-Zohar, Michael. "David Ben-Gurion: Prime Minister of Israel." *Encyclopaedia Britannica*, July 20, 1998. https://www.britannica.com/biography/David-Ben-Gurion.

BBC. "Arab Leaders Relaunch Peace Plan." March 28, 2007. http://news.bbc.co.uk/2/hi/middle_east/6501573.stm.

———. "Text: Beirut Declaration." March 28, 2002. http://news.bbc.co.uk/2/hi/world/monitoring/media_reports/1899395.stm.

Bisharat, George. "Israel and Palestine: A True One-State Solution." *Washington Post*, September 3, 2010. http://www.washingtonpost.com/wp-dyn/content/article/2010/09/02/AR2010090204665.html.

Bolton, John R. "The Three-State Option." *Washington Post*, January 5, 2009. http://www.washingtonpost.com/wp-dyn/content/article/2009/01/04/AR2009010401434.html.

Boshnaq, Mona, Sewell Chan, Irit Pazner Garshowitz, and Gaia Tripoli. "The Conflict in Jerusalem Is Distinctly Modern. Here's the History." *New York Times*, December 5, 2017. https://www.nytimes.com/2017/12/05/world/middleeast/jerusalem-history-peace-deal.html.

Churchill, Winston. "British White Paper of June 1922." Yale Law School, 1922. Accessed December 8, 2017. http://avalon.law.yale.edu/20th_century/balfour.asp.

Columbia Law School. "Readings on Citizenship and Nationality in Israel/Palestine." The Open University Project. Accessed December 28, 2017. http://www.law.columbia.edu/open-university-project/curricula/citizenshipnationalityisrael-palestine#_ftn10.

Economist. "The Hundred Years' War." January 8, 2009. http://www.economist.com/node/12899483.

Eldar, Akiva. "The State of Israel's Worst Missed Opportunity." *Haaretz*, March 26, 2012. https://www.haaretz.com/opinion/the-state-of-israel-s-worst-missed-opportunity-1.420707.

Epstein, Lawrence J. *Americans and the Birth of Israel*. Lanham, MD: Rowman & Littlefield, 2017.

Fisher, Max. "Israel's Dark Future." *Vox*, April 13, 2015. https://www.vox.com/2015/4/13/8390387/israel-dark-future.

Friedman, Thomas. *From Beirut to Jerusalem*. New York: Farrar, Straus & Giroux, 1989.

Frydenborg, Bryan E. "Encountering Dehumanization." *Jerusalem Post*, January 6, 2016. http://www.jpost.com/Opinion/Encountering-dehumanization-439617.

Halwani, Raja. "The One-State Solution." In *The Israeli-Palestinian Conflict: Philosophical Essays on Self-Determination, Terrorism and the One-State Solution*, by

Raja Halwani and Tomas Kapitan, pp. 198–245. New York: Springer, 2008.

Independent. "Secret Memo Shows Israel Knew Six Day War Was Illegal." Information Liberation, May 28, 2007. http://www.informationliberation.com/?id=22182.

International Committee of the Red Cross. "Treaties, State Parties and Commentaries." August 12, 1949. https://ihl-databases.icrc.org/applic/ihl/ihl.nsf/Treaty.xsp?documentId=AE2D398352C5B028C12563CD002D6B5C&action=openDocument.

International Court of Justice. "International Court of Justice (ICJ) Ruling on the Israeli Security Barrier ('Wall')." Zionism and Israel Information Center, July 9, 2004. http://www.zionism-israel.com/hdoc/ICJ_fence.htm.

Jacobs, Frank. "The Elephant in the Map Room." *New York Times*, August 7, 2012. https://opinionator.blogs.nytimes.com/2012/08/07/the-elephant-in-the-map-room.

Jacoby, Tami Amanda. *Bridging the Barrier: Israeli Unilateral Disengagement.* London, UK: Routledge, 2017.

Jewish Virtual Library. "British White Papers: Zionist Reaction to the White Paper (1939)." 1939. http://www.jewishvirtuallibrary.org/zionist-reaction-to-the-white-paper-of-1939.

———. "Egypt-Israeli Relations: Interim Peace Agreement (Sinai II)." September 1, 1975. http://www.jewishvirtuallibrary.org/egypt-israel-interim-peace-agreement-sinai-ii-september-1975.

———. "Establishment of Israel: The Declaration of the Establishment of the State of Israel." May 14, 1948. http://www.jewishvirtuallibrary.org/the-declaration-of-the-establishment-of-the-state-of-israel.

BIBLIOGRAPHY

———. "Israel-Palestinian Peace Process: Letters of Mutual Recognition." September 9, 1993. https://www.jewishvirtuallibrary.org/israel-palestinian-letters-of-mutual-recognition-september-1993.

———. "Israel's Wars and Operations: Operation Defensive Shield." Accessed December 21, 2017. http://www.jewishvirtuallibrary.org/operation-defensive-shield.

———. "The Partition Plan: Background & Overview." Accessed January 1, 2018. http://www.jewishvirtuallibrary.org/map-of-the-u-n-partition-plan.

Karkhar, Sonja. "The First Intifada: Historical Overview." American Muslims for Palestine, December 10, 2007. https://www.ampalestine.org/palestine-101/history/intifadas/first-intifada-historical-overview.

Lawrence, T. E. *Seven Pillars of Wisdom*. Oxford, UK: Private Edition, 1926.

Lieshout, Robert H. *Britain and the Arab Middle East: World War I and Its Aftermath*. New York: I. B. Tauris, 2016.

Lowery, George. "The Effects of Israel's West Bank Barrier: Hopelessness, Shattered Lives and Distrust, Says Cornell Scholar." *Cornell Chronicle*, July 10, 2008. http://news.cornell.edu/stories/2008/07/cornell-sociologist-studies-israels-west-bank-barrier.

Margolick, David. "Endless War." *New York Times*, May 4, 2008. http://www.nytimes.com/2008/05/04/books/review/Margolick-t.html.

Mathew, William M. "McMahon, Sykes, Balfour: Contradictions and Concealment in British Palestine Policy 1915-1917." Balfour Project, April 17, 2016. http://www.balfourproject.org/mcmahon-sykes-balfour-contradictions-and-concealments-in-british-palestine-policy1915-1917.

McGreal, Chris. "World Court Tells Israel to Tear Down Illegal Wall." *Guardian*, July 4, 2004. https://www.theguardian.com/world/2004/jul/10/israel3.

Melhem, Ahmad. "Israeli-Palestinian Water Pact Raises Hopes, Suspicions." *Al-Monitor*, July 25, 2017. https://www.al-monitor.com/pulse/originals/2017/07/israel-palestine-economic-peace-water-agreement.html#ixzz52qAWFQdK.

Morris, Benny. *1948: A History of the First Arab-Israeli War.* New Haven, CT: Yale University Press, 2008.

Nourallah, Riad. *Beyond the Arab Disease: New Perspectives on Politics and Culture.* Abindgon, UK: Routledge, 2006.

Oren, Michael B. *Six Days of War: June 1967 and the Making of the Modern Middle East.* New York: Ballantine Books, 2017.

Pappé, Ilan. *The Making of the Arab-Israeli Conflict 1947–1951.* New York: I. B. Tauris, 1994.

Ramakrishna, Prashanth. "'Everybody Comes from Somewhere': An Interview with Amos Oz." *Believer Logger*, October 20, 2016. https://logger.believermag.com/post/2016/10/20/everybody-comes-from-somewhere.

"The Return to Jerusalem: What Representatives of Muslim and Christian Communities Think of Zionism." *Le Matin*, March 1, 1919.

Samuel, Herbert. "The Future of Palestine." 1915. https://en.wikisource.org/wiki/The_Future_of_Palestine.

Segev, Tom. *One Palestine, Complete: Jews and Arabs Under the British Mandate.* Basingstoke, UK: Macmillan Publishers, 2001.

Shlaim, Avi. *The Iron Wall: Israel and the Arab World.* New York: W. W. Norton, 2001.

BIBLIOGRAPHY

United Nations. "Resolution 242 (1967)." November 13, 1967. https://undocs.org/S/RES/242(1967).

———. "United Nations Conciliation Commission for Palestine Letter Dated 29 August 1949." August 29, 1949. https://unispal.un.org/DPA/DPR/unispal.nsf/0/B8253BCBDBC87D798525753F005B08E8.

United Nations Security Council. "Resolution 2334." December 23, 2016. https://undocs.org/S/RES/2334(2016).

Uyar, Mesut, and Edward J. Erickson. *A Military History of the Ottomans: From Osman to Ataturk*. Santa Barbara, CA: ABC-CLIO, 2009.

Williams, Jennifer, and Sarah Wildman. "Trump's Recognition of Jerusalem as Israel's Capital, Explained." *Vox*, December 6, 2017. https://www.vox.com/world/2017/12/6/16741528/trump-jerusalem-speech-israel-tel-aviv.

World Bank. "Gaza Economy on the Verge of Collapse, Youth Unemployment Highest in the Region at 60 Percent." May 21, 2015. http://www.worldbank.org/en/news/press-release/2015/05/21/gaza-economy-on-the-verge-of-collapse.

Yale Law School. "British White Paper of 1939." 1939. http://avalon.law.yale.edu/20th_century/brwh1939.asp.

INDEX

Page numbers in **boldface** are illustrations.

Abdullah ibn
 Husayn, **25**, 25–26
Arafat, Yasser, 50, **51**, **84**
Arab-Israeli Wars
 1948, 7, 43, 46–47,
  57, 69–70, 90
 1956/Suez
  Crisis, 49–50, 52
 1967/Six-Day War, 7, **52**,
  52–57, 70, 74, 82,
  89, 90, **90**
 1969–70/War of
  Attrition, 56
 1973, 7, 56, 81
Arab League, 43, 85
Arab Peace Initiative, 85–86
Arabs, 7, 16, 18, 46, 56
 independent state for,
  19–22, 24–29, 38–39,
  67–69, 79, 86–87

Balfour Declaration, 21–
 23, 26–27, 44
Ben-Gurion, David, 28–
 29, 44–45, **45**
borders, **72–73**
 gain in territory for
  Israel, 7, 47, 53–54,
  69–71, 78, 90
 Green Line, 46–48,
  53, 59, 69–70
 implementation of
  two-state system
  and, 89–92
 of newly formed Israel, 42
 ongoing dispute, 8–9, **60–
  61**, 71

of Palestine, 64–69, **65**
 proposed for future
  Palestinian state, 79
 security barriers, 59,
  74–78, **77**, 92
British Mandate for Iraq,
 24, 26, 66
British Mandate for Palestine,
 7, 24–35, 38, **54**, 64–67

Camp David Accords, 83
Churchill, Winston,
 24–26, **25**, 66
civil war (1947–1948), 7, **8**,
 37, 42–43, 46–47, 69
civil war (2006), 63
Clinton, Bill, **84**

demographics, 9, 28, 67, 69

Egypt, 43, 46, 49, 52–54, 56,
 66, 69–71, 82–83, 92

Fatah, 63
Faysal ibn Husayn, 22–23, 26
France, 16, 19, 21, 24, 35,
 47, 49, 65–66
French Mandate for
 Syria, 24, 65–66

Gaza Strip, 8, 46, 52, 54–57,
 55, 59–63, 70–71, 74–
 75, 78–79, 83–86, **91**, 92
Geneva Conference
 (1973), **80**, 82
Germany, 19, 23, 31–35
Golan Heights, 54, 66, 70–71
Great Britain, 18–21, 47, 49
 anti-British
  sentiment, 36–37

INDEX

Mandate for Palestine, 7, 24–35, 38, 64–67
Green Line, 46–47, **47**, 53, 59, 70

Hamas, 63, 86–87, 89
Holocaust, 35–36, 38
Husayn ibn Ali, 19–22, **20**, 26

Intifadas, 57–59, 83, 89
Iraq, 24, 26, 43, 52–53, 66, 70
Islam/Muslims
    early history, 13–16
    in Southern Levant, 4–6, 16–18, 90
Israel, **5**, **55**
    independence/founding, 7, 40–43, **41**, 44–45, 69, 90
    size of, 71
Israeli Defense Force (IDF), 43, 45, 49–50, 52, **52**, 53, 58, 63, 81, **90**
Israeli-Palestinian conflict
    history of region, 10–16
    in present day, 73–75, 81–94
    roots of, 4–9, 19–30

Jerusalem, 4, 10, **11**, **13**, 16, **29**, 30, 38, 64, 83, 89, **90**
    civil war, **8**, **37**
    East Jerusalem, 43, 54, 70–71, 85, 90–91
    under international rule, 67, 90
Jewish Agency for Israel, 31, 44

Jewish National Council, 40, 44
Jordan, 26, 42–43, 46, 52–53, 56, 66, 69–70, 82, 84
Judaism/Jews
    Diaspora, 12
    early history, 10–12
    in Europe, 16–19, **17**, **32–33**, 31–35, 36–37
    Holocaust, 35–36, 38
    pogroms, 16, **17**, 17–18
    promise of homeland, 21–34, 38–39, 44, 66–69
    in Southern Levant, 4–6, 11, 16–18, **29**, 90

Knesset, 45, 46, 91

Lausanne Protocol, 48–49
Lawrence, T. E., 21, **25**, 26
League of Nations, 24, 38, 64
Lebanon, 43, 46, 65, 69–70, 83

McMahon, Henry, 19, 22, 26

natural resources, distribution of, 4, 74, 78–79
Nazis, 31–35, **32–33**, 36

Oslo Accords, 83, **84**
Ottoman Empire, 14, **15**, 16, 18–21, 44, 64

Palestinian National Authority (PNA), 62–63, 83
Palestinians, 7, **60–61**, **72–73**, **87**, **91**
    economic state, 59–61, 76, 79

loss of land, 7–8, 46–48, 53–54, 69–71

refugees, 46, **47**, 48, 50, 69–70, 85, 89

statehood for, 62–63, 67–69, 79, 86–87

Palestinian territories, 8, 43, 46, 49, 52, 54, **55**, 56–57, 59–62, 69–71, **72–73**, 79, 83–86, **91**

Palestine (historic), **5, 55**

British mandate and, 24–35, 38, 64–67

history of, 10–16, 64

immigration quotas, 28, 30–31, 34, 36–37

UNSCOP plan for partition, 38–40, 47–48, 67–69

war in, 7, **8, 37**, 39–40, 42–43, 46–47

Palestine (state), 86–87

global and UN recognition of, 85

Palestine Liberation Organization (PLO), 50–51, 56, 62–63, 82–83, 91

peace

attempts at, 9, 53–56, 58, 71, 81–94, **93**

barriers to, 89–92

possible solutions, 86–89

Poland, **32–33**, 35

protests, **60–61, 91**

Rabin, Yitzhak, 51, 83, **84**

security barriers, 59, 74–78, **77**, 92

settlements, Israeli, 71–76, 78, 89

Sharon, Ariel, 58

Southern Levant, 4, 6, 8

history of, 10–16

migration of Jews to, 16–17

split into two mandates, 24

Soviet Union, 35, 42, 53, 56, 82–83

Suez Crisis, 49–50, 52, 53

Sykes-Picot Agreement, 21, 23–24, 26

Syria, 7, 16, 43, 46, 52–54, 56, 64–65, 69–70, 82–83

Transjordan, 25–26, 66

United Nations, 38–39, 46–47, 49–50, 53, 67–69, 73–76, 85, 90–91

Resolution 242, 82–83, 89

United States, 18–19, 35, 42, 47, 49, 56, 82–83

UNSCOP plan, 38–40, 47–48, 67–69, **68**, 90

water resources, 74, **74**

Weizmann, Chaim, 26

West Bank, 8, 43, 46, 49, 52, 54, **55**, 57, 59, 62–63, 69–71, **72–73**, 74–75, 79, 83–86, 89, 92

Western Wall, 90, **90**

White Paper of 1939, 30, 36

World War I, 7, 19–21, 23, 26, 30, 44

World War II, 35, 36

Zionism, 31, 44, 50, 80

birth of, 18–19

Kate Shoup has written more than forty books and has edited hundreds more. When she's not working, Shoup loves to travel, watch IndyCar racing, ski, read, and ride her motorcycle. She lives in Indianapolis with her husband, her daughter, and their dog.